CHAPTER I

OVERVIEW: (FROM STEAM T

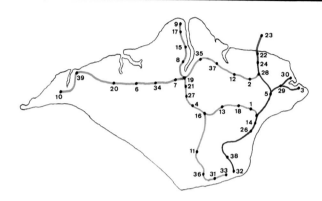

■ Isle of Wight Central Railway (IWC): 28¹/₄-route miles.
■ Isle of Wight Railway (IWR): 14 route miles.
■ Freshwater, Yarmouth & Newport Railway (FYN): 12-route miles.
■ Joint LSWR/LBSCR: 1¹/₄-route miles.

1: Alverstone. **2:** Ashey. **3:** Bembridge. **4:** Blackwater. **5:** Brading. **6:** Calbourne. **7:** Carisbrooke. **8:** Cement Mills Halt. **9:** Cowes. **10:** Freshwater. **11:** Godshill. **12:** Haven Street. **13:** Horringford. **14:** Lake. **15:** Medina Wharf & Halt. **16:** Merstone. **17:** Mill Hill. **18:** Newchurch. **19:** Newport. **20:** Ningwood. **21:** Pan Lane. **22:** Ryde Esplanade. **23:** Ryde Pier Head. **24:** Ryde St. Johns Road. **25:** Sandown. **26:** Shanklin. **27:** Shide. **28:** Smallbrook Junction. **29:** St. Helens. **30:** St. Helens Quay. **31:** St. Lawrence. **32:** Ventnor. **33:** Ventnor Town. **34:** Watchingwell. **35:** Whippingham. **36:** Whitwell. **37:** Wootton. **38:** Wroxall. **39:** Yarmouth.

NOTES

1: Ashey station closed 20.02.1966, but was re-opened by the Isle of Wight Steam Railway (IWSR) 02.05.1993.

12: Haven Street was originally one word, but officially became two in June 1958. The station closed 20.02.1966 but was re-opened by the IWSR 24.01.1971.

14: Lake Halt was open from 19.08.1889 until 1914; it was about ¹/₂ a mile south of the present station, which Network SouthEast opened on 09.07.1987.

15: Medina Wharf opened November 1878, and was rebuilt and enlarged by the Southern Railway. The Halt was opened circa 1909 (exact date unknown).

28: Smallbrook Junction station was opened by Network SouthEast 21.07.1991.

37: Wootton station closed 21.09.1953; the IWSR opened the present station (on a new site- east of the original) 31.05.1978.

Passenger Network Development.

Date.	Co.	Route.	Miles.	Total.
16.06.1862.	CNR.	Cowes-Newport.	$4^{1}/_{4}$	$4^{1}/_{4}$
23.08.1864.	IWR.	Ryde St. Johns-Shanklin.	$7^{1}/_{4}$	$11^{1}/_{2}$
10.09.1866.	IWR.	Shanklin-Ventnor.	4	$15^{1}/_{2}$
01.02.1875.	NJR.	Sandown-Shide.	$8^{1}/_{4}$	$23^{3}/_{4}$
06.10.1875.	NJR.	Shide-Pan Lane.	$^{1}/_{2}$	$24^{1}/_{4}$
20.12.1875.	RNR.	Smallbrook-Newport.	8	$32^{1}/_{4}$
01.06.1879.	NJR.	Pan Lane-Newport.	$^{1}/_{2}$	$32^{3}/_{4}$
05.04.1880.	JRC.	Ryde St. Johns-Ryde Esplanade.	$^{3}/_{4}$	$33^{1}/_{2}$
12.07.1880.	JRC.	Ryde Esplanade-Ryde Pier Head.	$^{1}/_{2}$	34
27.05.1882.	BHR.	Brading-Bembridge.	$2^{3}/_{4}$	$36^{3}/_{4}$
20.07.1889.	FYN.	Freshwater-Newport.	12	$48^{3}/_{4}$
20.07.1897.	NGS.	Merstone-St. Lawrence.	$5^{1}/_{2}$	$54^{1}/_{4}$
01.06.1900.	NGS.	St. Lawrence-Ventnor Town*.	$1^{1}/_{4}$	$55^{1}/_{2}$

Ventnor Town was renamed Ventnor West by the Southern Railway.

Company abbreviations.

BHR.   Brading Harbour Improvement & Railway Company.
CNR.   Cowes & Newport Railway.
FYN.   Freshwater, Yarmouth & Newport Railway.
IWC.   Isle of Wight Central Railway.
IWR.   Isle of Wight Railway.
JRC.   London & South Western Railway/London, Brighton & South Coast Railway. LSWR/LBSCR Joint Railway Companies.
NGS.   Newport, Godshill & St. Lawrence Railway.
NJR.   Isle of Wight (Newport Junction) Railway.
RNR.   Newport & Ryde Railway.

The Isle of Wight Central Railway (IWC).

The first railway to open on the Island was the $4^{1}/_{4}$-mile line from Cowes to Newport, owned by the Cowes & Newport Railway. They had two, blue painted Slaughter Gruning 2-2-2 tank locomotives, *Pioneer* and *Precursor,* to operate passenger only services, which commenced on Monday 16th June 1862.

On July 25th 1872 the Ryde & Newport Railway were authorised to build a railway between the two towns. At Ryde St. Johns Road, the IWR extended their station and laid track south to Smallbrook, the cost being shared by the two companies, and the CNR enlarged Newport station. The RNR line opened on Monday December 20th 1875, and in June 1876 the Directors of the RNR and the CNR, agreed to operate their two lines under a Joint Committee.

In 1868 the Isle of Wight (Newport Junction) Railway were authorised to build a railway from Sandown to Newport, via Merstone. The company faced financial problems from the outset, which led them to cut costs wherever they could, but in their worst nightmares the directors could not have imagined that the $9^{1}/_{4}$-mile line would open in three stages, and take 11 years to complete!

1556

Dedicated to Olwyn with all my love.

Stagecoach Island Line: Part of the National Rail Network.
w.w.w.island-line.com

ISLAND LINE

THE ISLE OF WIGHT'S AWARD WINNING ELECTRIC RAILWAY

In 1992 Ryde Depot was awarded ISO 9000 for train maintenance, and in 1998 Island Line Trains were awarded the prestigious Charter Mark, for customer services. The company regularly win top marks from the Strategic Rail Authority, for the reliability and punctuality of its train services.

CONTENTS

INTRODUCTION

Island Line is the story of the Isle of Wight's electric railway from Ryde to Shanklin. Starting with its opening in 1864, through its fight for survival, and the transition from steam to electric traction, in 1967. The reasons for using ex-London Underground trains are explained, with details of passenger and engineering stock. Finally, the reader is taken on an informative guided tour of the route.

The Isle of Wight could, at one time, boast a rail network of 55¹/₂ miles serving 36 stations, which took 38 years to develop. Due mainly to competition from road transport the network could not be sustained, infact it only lasted for 52 years. All that now remains is the 8¹/₂-mile line from Ryde to Shanklin, which is the subject of this book. In addition the Isle of Wight Steam Railway (IWSR) operate the very atmospheric 5-mile heritage line, from Smallbrook Junction to Wootton.

It is probably true to say that there have been more books written about the Isle of Wight railways, then any area on the north island (mainland), but virtually all of them have concentrated on the steam era. Whilst there is no doubt that steam is fondly remembered, and sorely missed, it has been over 35 years since the last steam train ran on Ryde Pier. A generation has only known the ex-London Underground trains that now ply the route however, by comparison, very little has been written about these unique trains. Hopefully my book will help re-dress the balance, and give an insight as to why Underground is now Overground.

Acknowledgements.
I wish to extend my sincere appreciation to the Management and all the Staff, at Island Line, for their co-operation during the preparation of this book. My thanks go to Director Alan Cracknell. General Manager Steve Wade and his assistant Kim Irwin. Ryde Depot Supervisor Jess Harper, and fitter Kevin

Weeks. I am deeply indebted to Conductor/Guard Phil Evans, for his photographs of the Class 485/486.

References.
Railways in the Wight. C.J. Whittington. (G.G. Saunders & Co, Shanklin). South Coast Railways-Ryde to Ventnor. Mitchell & Smith. (Middleton Press 1985. ISBN: 906520-19-3). Rails in the Isle of Wight. Allen & MacLeod (David & Charles 1986 ISBN: 0-7153-8701-4). The Isle of Wight Railway. Maycock & Silsbury. (The Oakwood Press 1999. ISBN: 0-85361-544-6). The Isle of Wight Railway Stock Book. (Isle of Wight Steam Railway Co Ltd 1994. ISBN: 0-9506-1543-9).

Underground (no. 11). London Underground Railway Society (LURS) 1983. Underground Train File Tube Stock 1933-1959. Brian Hardy. (Capital Transport 2001. ISBN: 185414-235-6). Tube Trains on the Isle of Wight. Brian Hardy. (Capital Transport 2003. ISBN: 185414-276-3). Motive Power Monthly Magazine (July 1986). Railway Magazine (April 1998). Rail Express Magazine (May 2005). Island Rail News Magazine (various). The Isle Of Wight County Press (various).

Track Diagrams.
The track diagrams are schematic to show how, over the years, the railway has rationalised to survive, combined with the mileage chart reasonably accurate model layouts could be achieved. Lengths of sidings and loops refer to clearance.

Island Line Passenger Train Models & Kits. (00 Gauge/4mm-ft).
Standard and 1938 stock (kits): Harrow Model Shop, 63 Station Road, Harrow, Middlesex. HA2 7SR. 1938 stock (model): Exclusive First Editions. 32 Woodall Road, Enfield. EN3 4LG. Motorising Kits: Branchlines, PO Box 31, Exeter, EX4 6NY. Lighting kits: First Class Trains, 221 Galmington Road, Taunton. TA1 4ST.

Ralph Humphries Carisbrooke Isle of Wight.
September 2003 & August 2005.

The 8¹/₄ miles from Sandown to Shide opened on February 1st 1875, followed by the ¹/₂-mile section to Pan Lane 8 months later on October 16th, the Isle of Wight Railway operated all the services, on behalf of the NJR. In 1878 the two companies became embroiled in a protracted argument, over the rental for using Sandown station, and the cost of repairs carried out on rolling stock, which amounted to £400. As a result the IWR decided to stop operating the line in early 1879, to make matters worse the NJR had been made bankrupt, building the substantial viaduct over the River Medina to reach Newport station.

An Official receiver appointed the joint CNR/RNR management to take over the operation of the route, from April 1st 1879, by which time goods trains were running over the viaduct, but it was not until a month later, on June 1st that passenger services commenced. This managerial situation lasted for 8 years, until July 1st 1887, when the three companies merged completely to form the Isle of Wight Central Railway.

On Monday 19th July 1897 the IWC started operating a new 5¹/₂-mile line, from Merstone to St. Lawrence, on behalf of the Newport, Godshill & St. Lawrence Railway (NGS). It had been intended that the line would reach Ventnor, but it took another three years to build the 1¹/₄-mile extension, which opened on June 1st 1900, the last new railway to be built on the Island. The railway was purchased by the IWC on October 1st 1913, for £36,000, this made the IWC the largest of the Island rail companies, with 28¹/₄-route miles.

The Isle of Wight Railway (IWR).

The Isle of Wight (Eastern Section) Railway was authorised, on July 23rd 1860 to construct a railway from Ryde to Ventnor, via Bonchurch. However, due to local opposition the route was changed to run to Ventnor via Wroxall. This revised route required a 1,312-yard tunnel, south of Wroxall, under St. Boniface Down.

Due to lengthy delays constructing the tunnel the line opened in two stages, the 7¹/₄-mile section from Ryde to Shanklin opened to passenger services on Tuesday 23rd August 1864, by which time the company had shortened its name to the Isle of Wight Railway. In addition there was a ¹/₂-mile goods only line, from Brading to Brading Quay, freight services commenced four months later, in December.

The 4-mile extension from Shanklin to Ventnor officially opened on Monday 10th September 1866, at which time Wroxall station was not completed (it opened later in the year), and Ventnor station was described as a 'wretched place'.

From February 1st 1875 the IWR started operating services for the Newport Junction Railway, from Sandown to Pan Lane. The two companies had many disagreements that led to a parting of the ways four years later, in 1879, just before the line eventually opened throughout to Newport.

Meanwhile, on August 7th 1874 the Brading Harbour Improvement Railway & Works Company was incorporated to construct the 2³/₄-mile branch, from Brading to Bembridge, this new railway formed an end on junction with the IWR line at Brading Quay. It was estimated that the cost would be in the region of £40,000, including the provision of new quays at St. Helens, to replace those at Brading.

On August 1st 1878 the line was opened as far as St. Helens Quay, for goods traffic only, which the IWR operated. The embankment between St. Helens and Bembridge proved very difficult to complete, and a partial collapse cost an extra £10,000 to repair, with the work being completed in February 1880.

The BHR were financially embarrassed, and lapsed into receivership from June 1881. In February 1882, the IWR agreed to operate the line as part of their system, for 50% of the gross receipts, and three months later on Saturday 27th May 1882 the branch to Bembridge was opened to passenger traffic.

The company changed its name to the Brading Harbour Railway on August 14th 1896, and on July 31st 1898 the company was purchased by the IWR, for a total of £16,500. The IWR now had 14-route miles making them the second largest and, eventually, the most successful of the Island railway ventures.

The Freshwater, Yarmouth & Newport Railway (FYN).

On September 10th 1888 the 12-mile line from Freshwater to Newport was opened, to goods traffic only; it was not until July 11th 1889 that passenger services commenced. The FYN had a working agreement with the Isle of Wight Central Railway, who provided the rolling stock, and operated the services, the FYN were responsible for maintenance of the route, through their contractor.

The two companies had many disputes over the years about the stock provided, and rent for using Newport station, matters came to a head in 1913 when the FYN decided to go it alone. They purchased their own locomotives and rolling stock, and opened their own station at Newport, 200 yards from the IWC station.

Independent operations commenced on July 1st 1913, by that time the FYN were bankrupt! Agreement was reached which allowed some FYN trains to use the IWC station, but they remained independent (and bankrupt) for the next 10 years.

The Ryde Pier Company (RPC).

In addition to the railways, trams operated by the RPC played an important role for 105 years. In July 1812 the RPC were authorised to construct a promenade pier, at Ryde, which took two years to complete. Over the following years that pier was extended several times, eventually it reached 2,250 feet out into the Solent, beyond the extensive sand banks, so that ships could reach it at any state of tide.

It was not long before ferry services to Portsmouth commenced, followed by other vessels offering Solent cruises. So many people were using the pier the RPC gained approval to build a second structure; the work commenced in 1863, and took one year to complete. The RPC laid two standard gauge tramlines, on this pier, and horse drawn trams started on Monday August 29th 1864.

In November 1865 the RPC applied to extend the tramlines to the IWR station, at St. Johns Road, but for 4 years they were refused permission. It was not until June 5th 1869 that work started which was completed in two stages, the first in 1870, with the entire route opening on August 1st 1871. The tramlines formed an end on junction with the IWR track, which required a level crossing on St. Johns Road. Passengers transferred to the trams, for the journey to and from the pier.

During 1880 the trams reverted to pier only operation, when the LSWR/LBSCR opened their new line, giving through rail services to the new Pier Head station. From 1881 steam trams operated but from November 1st 1884 horse drawn trams were used again. In October 1885 the tramlines were electrified, using a third rail system, which started operating in March 1886.

LSWR/LBSCR Joint Railway Companies.

The London & South Western Railway, and the London, Brighton & South Coast Railway both operated services from Portsmouth to London, and they felt that the lack of a proper rail link from St. Johns Road to the ferries was having an adverse effect on the growth of their services. It was obvious that the Island companies could not, or would not build that important missing link.

The LSWR/LBSCR formed a Joint Company with the intention of building a new pier; linked by rail to St. Johns Road station, work on the £250,000 project commenced in 1878. An overbridge replaced the level crossing at St. Johns Road, and other bridges were also required for Rink Road and Park Road. In addition a 391-yard cut and cover tunnel was constructed at Ryde Esplanade, due to pressure from locals who apparently disliked the idea of having a level crossing!

On April 5th 1880 the section from St. Johns Road to the Esplanade opened, followed three months later on July 12th, by the section to Ryde Pier Head. The route was laid to double track, and operated by the IWR and the RNR (later the IWC). So that approaching trains could be easily recognised, IWR trains carried a white disc with a green centre, or a green lamp, on the front of the locomotive.

To maximise on their investment, the LSWR/LBSCR also purchased the Port of Portsmouth & Ryde Steam Packet Company, and its 7 ships, in a deal worth £38,000. The company was immediately renamed The Joint Railway Steam Packet Company, which started operations in April 1880.

Southern Railway (SR).

From January 1st 1923 the railways of Britain were grouped, into the 'Big 4', The Great Western Railway (GWR), The London & North Eastern (LNER), London, Midland & Scottish (LMS), and the Southern Railway (SR). The Island companies (including the LSWR/LBSCR line and rail owned ferry services) came under the newly created Southern, except the FYN, which was absorbed 7 months later.

Grouping was achieved through a compulsory amalgamation programme, but the directors of the FYN felt that the level of compensation was inadequate. The dispute was referred to an Amalgamation Tribunal, who settled the compensation at £50,000, which led to the FYN being absorbed during August 1923.

In 1924 the Southern Railway purchased the Ryde Pier Company, and in November 1927 they replaced the electric system with petrol driven trams.

The Southern invested extensively across the Island, replacing locomotives and rolling stock; the more heavily used former IWR line saw the most investment. Smallbrook Junction was created (1926), the track between Brading-Sandown was doubled (1927) and Ryde Pier Head station enlarged (1933). Platforms along the route were all lengthened to take 6-carriage trains.

British Railways (BR).

From January 1st 1948, the 'Big 4' were nationalised, with Island services coming under the Southern Region of British Railways. BR did invest in the Island, but it was not long before a closure programme was introduced.

Date.	Route Closed.	Miles.	Remaining Miles.
15.09.1952.	Merstone-Ventnor West.	6³/₄	48³/₄
21.09.1953.	Freshwater-Newport.	12	36³/₄
21.09.1953.	Brading-Bembridge.	2³/₄	34
06.02.1956.	Sandown-Newport.	9¹/₄	24³/₄
20.02.1966.	Smallbrook-Cowes.	12¹/₄	12¹/₂
18.04.1966.	Shanklin-Ventnor.	4	8¹/₂

Note: Goods only traffic continued to St. Helens Quay until November 1957. Medina Wharf to Cowes and Shanklin to Ventnor until 16.05.1966. Medina Wharf to Smallbrook was retained for works/electrification trains until 20.10.1966.

During 1959-60 the petrol trams were converted to diesel and over the winter months of 1963-64 Ryde Pier was extensively repaired, with new timber decking. On September 17th 1966 Ryde Pier head station closed, temporarily, to allow the station to be reduced from four roads to two. Trains terminated at the Esplanade, where passengers transferred to the trams for the journey along the pier.

The end of steam, and all goods traffic came on December 31st 1966, the last passenger train left Shanklin at 22.12 hauled by Adams 02 number 14 *Fishbourne*, (built in 1889) which was the oldest locomotive regularly working on British Rail.

The Electric Era.

As far back as 1960 BR had been discussing what to do with the Island network; stock was well passed its sell by date, and the infrastructure worn out. Due to the restricted clearance of the tunnel and bridges in the Ryde area, and the severity of the curve through the Esplanade station, mainland stock could not be used.

The answer came from London Transport, which had some aging stock for sale; at little more then scrap value. British Rail allocated £500,000 to modernise and electrify the 8½-mile route, from Ryde Pier Head to Shanklin, which also included the cost of the rolling stock. Initially BR prepared a total of 43 cars, which were converted for use on the Island at London Transport and BR workshops, in addition a replacement car was prepared by LT, which was delivered to the Island in 1971.

Surprisingly (perhaps), this was not the first time that electrification had been mooted, in 1909 it had been suggested that the entire network should be converted, which would have cost in the region of £310,000. It was not the first time either that ex-London stock had come to the former Isle of Wight Railway route, in 1897/98 the IWR had purchased 10 carriages from the North London Railway, and in 1914 they purchased 18 carriages from the Metropolitan Railway.

This row of beach huts on the Duver at St. Helens is, infact, the remains of the 18 ex-Metropolitan Railway carriages purchased by the IWR in 1914, for a total of £874. They were all withdrawn, between June 1928 and April 1929. 14.03.99.

Preparation of the route commenced in January 1966, and took 15 months to complete. Ryde Pier Head station was reduced from four to two roads, with track rationalisation taking place along the entire route, including the removal of the cross over to the north of the Esplanade station. The track bed was raised through the stations, so as to avoid a big step down from the platforms, except at Ryde Esplanade where the platforms were lowered, as the track was partly on the pier.

British Rail announced that there would be an hourly service during the winter, increased to half hourly on weekdays during the summer, with 5 trains per hour on summer Saturdays. In addition fares would be restructured with some increases.

Revised Fares:

From.	To.	1967. Single.	Return.	1966. Single.	Return.
Pier Head.	Esplanade.	6d (2¹/₂p)		4d	
Esplanade.	Brading.	2/0d	2/0d (10p)	1/4d	1/10d
	Sandown.	2/6d	2/6d (12¹/₂p)	2/0d	2/9d
	Shanklin.	3/0d	3/0d (15p) 2/3d	3/0d	

Trial running on the St. Johns Road-Shanklin section started on Saturday 4th March 1967, a 7-car train making four return trips daily. Trials on the northern section to Ryde Pier Head commenced 11 days later, on Wednesday 15th March.

The electric era started on Monday 20th March 1967 with a basic hourly service, in addition at 12:18 a 'special' service left the Pier Head, with BR managers the Island MP, and other invited guests. The train ran to Shanklin, where a launch day luncheon was held at the Shanklin Hotel, before they were returned to Ryde.

The new service exceeded all expectations, with more passengers being carried then during the steam era, thoughts quickly turned to re-opening the section from Shanklin-Ventnor. However, it was estimated that it would cost around £100,000, so the re-opening was not authorised. In retrospect what a bargain that would have been, thirty years later the cost had increased to a staggering £10 million!

On January 26th 1969 Ryde Pier tramway closed, after 105 years of service, a train was used to operate a pier shuttle, when required. The shuttle carried passengers from the Pier Head to the Esplanade, and then continued empty to St. Johns Road, where it crossed to the up line and returned to the Esplanade. This necessitated the peak mainline service being reduced from five trains to 4 per hour, but still gave an intensive 5-train service on the busy Ryde Pier section.

In 1973 it was found that the scissor crossing, at Ryde Pier Head, was worn out but the cost of replacing it was deemed too high. At the same time the Pier Head signal box was found to be in a dangerous state of repair, as a result bi-directional working on the former up line (number 1 road) was introduced in October 1973.

The scissor crossing was replaced by plain track, and a new trailing cross over was installed to the south of the Esplanade station, two-aspect colour light signals controlled the section replacing the last semaphore signals on the pier.

This new layout meant that the pier shuttle train could be isolated on number 2 road, thus negating the empty journey to and from Ryde St. Johns, to rejoin the up line. Ryde St. Johns Road signal box assumed control of the section on May 5th 1974, the Pier Head box remained closed and was demolished later that year.

In 1985 the route became known as 'Ryde Rail', and one year later on June 10th 1986 Network SouthEast was launched, its area of operation included the Isle of Wight. To introduce the new company 'Ryde Rail Day' was held on June 21st, with the Depot being open to the public. NSE livery was applied to 24 cars, between January 1987 and May 1989. Digital clocks appeared at the Pier Head, Esplanade and Shanklin stations, and NSE red was applied to all platform lamps and seats.

NSE were also responsible for opening two new stations on the route, Lake opened on July 9th 1987, in a joint initiative with the Isle of Wight County Council. Smallbrook Junction station opened on July 20th 1991, to provide a cross-platform connection with the award winning Isle of Wight Steam Railway (IWSR).

In 1988 NSE announced that they were going to reduce the double track between Brading and Sandown, to single line. The Southern had doubled this section of track, which had opened on June 23rd 1927, in time for the summer. This cost cutting also led to the closure of the signal boxes, at both stations, leaving only Ryde St. Johns Road operational to control the entire 8¹/₂-mile route.

Work started straight away, with both boxes duly closing on October 29th 1988 however, an electrical fault led to Sandown box re-opening the next day. After a new cable was laid, Sandown box finally closed on February 5th 1989, and it was demolished one year later, when a wooden fence was erected on the platform.

During 1989 Network SouthEast introduced a new form of Line Management, which resulted in 19 regional route brandings, such as West of England and Solent & Wessex. As a result, from May 15th 1989, Ryde Rail became NSE's Island Line.

Network SoutEast's most important decision was to replace the trains once again, however, they were aged ex-London Underground tube trains, the 1938 Stock was already 50 years old! A total of 20 cars were delivered to the Island between July 5th 1989 and April 9th 1992, 18 for service use with two spares.

On December 4th 1993 the Rail Privatisation Bill was passed by Parliament and, as a result, British Rail passenger services were divided into 25 Train Operating Units (TOU's); and from April 1st 1994 the route became Island Line. The units were then vested as Limited Companies, known as Train Operating Companies (TOC's); which led to the creation of Island Line Ltd on December 10th 1995.

In the meantime car 125 collided with the buffers at Ryde Pier Head, on February 10th 1994, and was withdrawn. A further five cars were withdrawn between December 16th 1994 and June 28th 1996, leaving just six trains in service.

It was announced on September 26th 1996 that Stagecoach Holdings, who officially took over the route at 02:00 on Sunday 13th October 1996, had won the Island Line Ltd franchise. Stagecoach lease the six trains (12 cars) from HSBC Rail for around £149,000 per annum. Initially for a five-year period, the franchise has been extended until February 2007, while the future of the line is decided.

On November 2nd 2004 the Strategic Rail Authority, with Government backing set up a Community Railway Project, under the auspices of the Association of Community Rail Partnerships (ACoRP). By May 2005, 56 lines (around 1154 route miles and 390 stations) including Island Line had been nominated for assessment and, if they meet the criteria, will officially be designated as a Community Railway. The chosen lines must have backing from the local planning authority, and have a strong support organisation, with the active involvement of the local community.

The idea of this project is to reduce overheads, and the level of Government subsidy, by introducing innovative local projects to increase revenue. On Saturday 12th May 2005 the first 'Community Rail Day' was staged at some of the designated lines. Island Line introduced discounted fares, and nearby tourist attractions offered reduced admission charges, to Island Line ticket holders.

The first meeting of the Island Line Community Rail partnership was held at Winchester House, Sandown, on June 20th 2005. This partnership includes Portsmouth Harbour station and the Lymington branch line, both operated by South West Trains (owned by Stagecoach Holdings) and Wightlink Ferries as they all contribute heavily in bringing passengers to the Island. The Isle of Wight Council, and other interested transport operators are also included.

Island Line carries around 1 million passengers per year, but it remains the most heavily subsidised route on the National Rail Network (around £17 per passenger journey), but it plays a vitally important role for Island public transport.

In 2004 an Office of National Statistics survey revealed that of the 54,483 daily commuters, 3.9% use Island Line trains, incredibly this is the same percentage that use Island-wide bus services, but a massive 54% use their car! Island roads can barely cope with local traffic, let alone the annual influx of tourist vehicles, arriving on larger ferries. The route desperately needs, and deserves, continued investment to help prevent Island roads becoming totally grid locked!

CHAPTER 2

PASSENGER TRAINS - LT STANDARD STOCK (BR CLASS 485/486).

At the dawn of the 1960's the Island had a fleet of non-corridor carriages that had come from the London, Brighton & South Coast Railway and the South East & Chatham Railway, with around 500 various wagons. There were 19 Adams 02 class locomotives, with an average age of 74. If the remaining 25 route miles, with their restricted clearances, were to remain open something had to be done-but what?

BR considered increasing the clearances to take mainland stock, which would have cost around £1 million, or the purchase of purpose built new stock, estimated at approximately £915,000. In 1961 BR spoke to London Transport (LT) with a proposal to buy 65 tube cars, which would be formed into block trains, operated with push-pull power cars, as a replacement for the aging steam locomotives and carriages. The cheapest option, of course, was to close the remaining lines!

On March 25th 1963 the Beeching Report recommended that the Island network, with the exception of the 1¼-mile section from Ryde Pier Head to Ryde St. Johns Road, should be closed. As a result BR spoke to LT again, stating that just two Driving Motors (DM) and four trailers (TR) would be required.

LT agreed to sell the six cars for a total of £1,040, £280 each for the DM's (which would have no traction motors), and £120 each for the TR's. BR was considering converting the driving cars with diesel-mechanical Gardiner engines, which local bus company Southern Vectis, had agreed to maintain. The Vectis Bus Company had been purchased by the Southern Railway, in March 1929, and had subsequently been renamed Southern Vectis to reflect railway ownership.

In the summer of 1965, following a long and spirited 'Save Our Railways' campaign, Mr Fraser MP Minister of Transport announced that the 8½-mile section from Ryde Pier Head to Shanklin was to remain open. It was also stated that the route was to be modernised, and the line electrified. The total cost of the project was £500,000, approximately 25% for stock acquisition and conversion, with the balance used on route rationalisation and preparation.

In November 1965 BR purchased 46 cars, included 4 spares, costing £14,860, and five months later preparation of the stock commenced, at London Transport's Acton Works. This included overhauling electrical and braking equipment, and conversion of the power cars from LT four-rail system to run on BR's standard Southern Region three-rail system, which was estimated to cost a further £89,000.

BR also proposed preparing the stock for one-person-operation, but this had to be discounted due to cost, estimated at an extra £1,000 for every cab conversion. Three types of car were purchased for the Island project, Driving Motors (DM) classified as either A or D, Control Trailers (CT), which had a driving cab but no motors and Trailers (TR). Standard (pre-1938) tube stock was the largest group on the Underground, with 1,466 cars ordered over a 12-year period (1922-1934), which comprised 645 Driving Motors, 270 Control Trailers and 551 Trailers.

The cost of preparation proved more expensive then estimated, so BR considered not having the four spare cars, which would save £9,000, or running 6-car trains instead of 7-car, saving £8,000. In September 1966 BR decided to reduce their requirement to 43 cars, 42 for service with only one spare Driving Motor (A), which resulted in three cars being renumbered. (Please see page 20).

Converted stock was transferred to BR's Stewart Lane Depot (via Wimbledon) for painting in 12 movements, between May 13th 1966 and February 16th 1967, comprising 7 rakes of four cars and 5 rakes of three cars. These trains were the first complete train sets in the new BR Corporate blue livery, with yellow cab ends, complete with white double arrow logos (arrows of indecision) and numbers.

The cars were fitted with luggage racks, which took the place of some seating; Driving Motors had one rack replacing 3 seats. Control Trailers and Trailers each got two racks, replacing 6 seats, the window behind the racks were plated over. Between January 1981 and August 1986 the interior of 33 cars were painted lime green and white, replacing the original mushroom and white scheme. Phil Evans.

The Driving Motors (DM) were classified as either A or D, due to differing types of couplings, the A car was always at the Ryde end of the train. DM (D) S7 entered service with LT as number 3209 on 13.03.33; it was withdrawn in November 1966. It was transferred to BR in February 1967, and entered Island service on 26.04.67. It was withdrawn in September 1990, and returned to the mainland one month later, and is now preserved with the LT Heritage Train Project. Phil Evans.

12

Converted stock undertook trials, between Wimbledon and Woking, before transferring to Fratton Depot (on the outskirts of Portsmouth), from where Island crews were given type training on the main line between Fratton and Haslemere.

Cranes were used to lift the cars onto Pickford's low loaders, until special ramps were installed, for onward travel to Ryde St. Johns Road. While at Fratton, Driving Motor (A) S22S was hit by some mainline stock, which caused damage to the windscreens, door pillars and lights, none of which was too serious. It was taken to the Island and repaired at Ryde Depot, before entering service.

I was unable to ascertain delivery dates to the Island (or the date that set 041 entered traffic), but on September 1st 1966 the first car arrived, via the Portsmouth-Fishbourne car ferry. Control Trailer (A) S38S (later S26S) was delivered to Ryde St. Johns Road for unloading and, three days later took part in clearance trials between Ryde and Shanklin, hauled by steam locomotive 24 *Calbourne*. Due to the different types of couplings, a wagon fitted with both types (known as a match truck), was marshalled between the locomotive and the car.

During subsequent stock deliveries at Ryde, two trailers were damaged, when S46S ran down the ramp and collided with S49S. This resulted in slight damage to the couplings and underframe of both cars, which was repaired at Ryde Depot.

The stock was marshalled into six 4-car units (numbered 041-046) classified 4VEC, and six 3-car sets (numbered 031-036) classified 3TIS. During peak periods these could be combined to form a 7-car VECTIS, the identification derived from the Roman name for the Isle of Wight. Initially 7-car trains were formed by like numbered sets (i.e. 041 with 031), until stock withdrawals made this impossible.

After 5 months of service, the trains were causing a major problem with excessive wheel flange and rail wear, resulting from the difference in gauge, the BR standard is 4'8½" whereas LT uses 4'8¾". This problem was so severe that line speed was reduced from 45 to 30 miles per hour, with just 10mph over all points.

The fitting of some checkrails to stop side play, and the installation of wheel flange lubricators cured the problem, allowing the speed limits to be returned to normal. It is interesting to note that during the steam era the maximum speed was 40 miles per hour, while the electric stock are allowed to do 45 mph.

The new service was proving so successful that BR considered re-opening the Shanklin-Ventnor line, and in October 1967 LT offered to sell 7 cars. Unfortunately the project was finally cancelled due to costs, estimated at £100,000, which included a new electric sub-station, track upgrading, and station refurbishment.

During the autumn of 1967, DM (D) S15S was badly damaged at Ryde Depot, while undergoing maintenance. It had been standing on blocks when it was knocked off by other stock, during a shunting manoeuvre that went wrong! Damage was estimated at £3,500, while LT quoted £4,300 for a replacement car.

BR wanted to close the tram service, and replace it with a 7-car train, but that would have cost £7,400, which was not authorised. Instead the tram service was closed on January 26th 1969, and a 7-car train formed the pier shuttle, but with no replacement stock the peak service on the mainline was reduced, from five trains per hour to four. It was also in 1969 that the trains were given class numbers, which were not displayed; the 3TIS became class 451 and the 4VEC class 452.

Eventually BR authorised a replacement for S15S, which was the only car to be painted by London Transport, it was delivered in 1971 having been renumbered S15S. The rest of the stock was re-painted at Ryde during 1971-72, as the dark blue had badly faded to a chalky blue; at the same time the S suffix was discontinued (i.e. S15S became S15). The car interiors were repainted the following year, all of the work being carried out at Ryde Depot.

On September 10th 1973 trains 035 and 045 collided, while they were out of passenger service, at Ryde St. Johns Road station. Three cars (S23/45/48) from 045 had to be scrapped, the remaining Driving Motor (A) S6

The Metropolitan Carriage & Wagon Co built Control Trailer S28, in 1925. It arrived on the Island February 27th 1967, and entered traffic on March 20th, in set 032. It was used as a trailer, but in January 1987 the cab was re-instated, making it the only Control Trailer used as such, on the Island. It gained Network SouthEast livery at the same time, one of 24 cars to obtain these colours. It was withdrawn on May 31st 1991, and was scrapped at Sandown in April 1994. Phil Evans.

Cammell Laird & Co built Trailer S49 in 1923; it was withdrawn by LT as number 7296, in 1964. This was one of the two cars damaged at Ryde, when S46 ran down the unloading ramp, having been repaired it entered traffic on March 20th 1967. It was withdrawn in September 1990, and returned to the mainland on October 2nd, for use in the London Transport Heritage Train Project. Phil Evans.

was transferred to set 035 (cars S9/24/95) which was then renumbered 045. Set 036 was subsequently renumbered 035, so that there was no gap in the numbering sequence.

It was also during 1973 that the trains were re-classified, class 451 became 486, and class 452 became 485. The class numbers were not displayed on the stock until 1982, when the trains were painted in Inter City blue and grey livery.

On September 8th 1975 car S25 (set 046) was severely damaged by fire, at Ryde St. Johns, it was withdrawn and scrapped 7 years later. The remaining cars (S8/46/49) were used as spares until 1980, when the set was renumbered 036.

In 1985 the remaining stock was completely reformed, into five 5-car trains (041-045) and two 2-car trains (031-032). It was also during 1985 that modifications were made to the front of the Driving Motors. The doors on the front of the cabs had been a constant source of discomfort for the Island drivers, with excessive draughts, and the ingress of water causing the cab to flood.

The doors were panelled over, at Ryde Depot, to give a smoother and weatherproof front. Car S5 (from set 043) was the first treated, the work being completed by June 6th 1985, a further 13 cars were modified by June 1988.

At the same time the route was re-branded as Ryde Rail, which was displayed on the new front panel. The legend 'Ryde Rail-Isle of Wight' was also displayed on the side of the Driving Motor cars, using white lettering.

In 1986 Network SouthEast took responsibility for the route and, from January 1987, some of the remaining stock was repainted into the striking new livery, nicknamed 'toothpaste' (due to its similarity to Aquafresh). In 1988 NSE announced replacement of the Standard stock, some of which was 65 years old!

DM (D) 9 has been painted into Network SouthEast livery, which in my opinion suited the stock best; the striking new colours were applied to 24 cars between January 1987 and May 1989. NSE stopped using the S prefix, when cars were painted, so S9 became 9. This car has also had the front-end modification, with NSE/Ryde Rail logos (compare with the lower view on page 12). Phil Evans.

Upper: On 28.09.89 four cars were returned to the mainland including car 29, which is being lifted onto a low loader, at Sandown. It was scrapped a year later. *Lower:* Car 9 (on the lorry) returned to the mainland on 13.03.90, followed by car 11 three days later, both went to LT for parts recovery. Both: Phil Evans.

Standard Stock Finale.

Cars 5/28/31 made the last recorded revenue earning runs, on January 12th 1991. Car 31 had been fitted with de-icing equipment in 1971/72; the last run on such duties was on February 17th 1991. The trio were finally withdrawn on May 13th 1991, and they were scrapped at Sandown in April 1994, by Gwent Demolition.

Standard Stock: Mainland Service Details.

BR No.	LT No.	Type.	Maker.	Year.	In Service.	Withdrawn.	LT-BR.
S1S.	3703.	DM/D.	MCW.	1934.	05.01.35.	07.1964.	29.09.66.
S2S.	3706.	DM/A.	MCW.	1934.	01.06.35.	07.1964.	20.10.66.
S3S.	3251.	DM/D.	MCW.	1931.	30.09.32.	10.1966.	05.01.67.
S4S.	3702.	DM/A.	MCW.	1934.	04.04.35.	07.1964.	08.07.66.
S5S.	3185.	DM/D.	MCW.	1931.	09.01.33.	10.1966.	26.01.67.
S6S.	3084.	DM/A.	MCW.	1931.	04.02.32.	08.1966.	07.11.66.
S7S.	3209.	DM/D.	MCW.	1931.	13.03.33.	11.1966.	16.02.67.
S8S.	3074.	DM/A.	MCW.	1931.	06.10.32.	06.1964.	29.09.66.
S9S.	3223.	DM/D.	MCW.	1931.	05.01.33.	11.1966.	16.02.67.
S10S.	3696.	DM/A.	MCW.	1934.	17.01.35.	10.1966.	26.01.67.
S11S.	3705.	DM/D.	MCW.	1934.	18.01.35.	08.1966.	07.11.66.
S12S.	Renumbered S22S before entering service on the Island.						
S13S.	3141.	DM/D.	MCW.	1931.	18.09.32.	06.1963.	08.09.66.
S15S.	3253.	DM/D.	MCW.	1931.	20.09.32.	06.1964.	20.10.66.
S15S.	3273.	DM/D.	MCW.	1931.	31.08.32.	08.1964.	20.03.71.
S17S.	Renumbered S21S before entering service on the Island.						
S19S.	3045.	DM/D.	UCC.	1928.	06.05.29.	10.1964.	10.06.66.
S20S.	3308.	DM/A.	UCC.	1928.	22.11.29.	10.1964.	08.09.66.
S21S.	3041.	DM/D.	UCC.	1928.	26.04.29.	10.1964.	18.08.66.
S22S.	3010.	DM/A.	UCC.	1929.	14.10.30.	10.1964.	13.05.66.
S23S.	3315.	DM/D.	MCW.	1927.	26.08.29.	10.1964.	08.07.66.
S25S.	3313.	DM/D.	MCW.	1927.	15.07.29.	10.1964.	13.05.66.
S26S.	5294.	CT/A.	MCW.	1925.	13.09.26.	10.1964.	10.06.66.
S27S.	5279.	CT/D.	MCW.	1926.	09.09.26.	10.1964.	08.09.66.
S28S.	5304.	CT/A.	MCW.	1925.	17.10.26.	10.1964.	01.12.66.
S29S.	5293.	CT/D.	MCW.	1925.	13.09.26.	10.1964.	29.09.66.
S30S.	5312.	CT/A.	MCW.	1925.	24.10.66.	10.1964.	05.01.67.
S31S.	5283.	CT/D.	MCW.	1925.	19.09.26.	10.1964.	20.10.66.
S32S.	5290.	CT/A.	MCW.	1925.	29.09.26.	10.1964.	05.01.67.
S33S.	5291.	CT/D.	MCW.	1925.	14.10.26.	10.1964.	18.08.66.
S34S.	5302.	CT/A.	MCW.	1925.	10.10.26.	10.1964.	26.01.67.
S36S.	5350.	CT/A.	MCW.	1927.	24.06.29.	10.1964.	18.08.66.
S38S.	Renumbered S26S before entering service on the Island.						
S41S.	7286.	TR.	CLC.	1923.	26.03.24.	10.1964.	08.08.66.
S42S.	7280.	TR.	CLC.	1923.	01.04.24.	10.1964.	29.09.66.
S43S.	7275.	TR.	CLC.	1923.	28.01.24.	10.1964.	20.10.66.
S44S.	7281.	TR.	CLC.	1923.	01.04.24.	10.1964.	08.07.66.
S45S.	7293.	TR.	CLC.	1923.	26.03.24.	10.1964.	17.11.66.
S46S.	7283.	TR.	CLC.	1923.	08.04.24.	10.1964.	13.05.66.
S47S.	7279.	TR.	CLC.	1923.	01.04.24.	10.1964.	10.06.66.
S48S.	7298.	TR.	CLC.	1923.	11.03.24.	10.1964.	17.11.66.
S49S.	7296.	TR.	CLC.	1923.	12.03.24.	10.1964.	13.05.66.
S92S.	7285.	TR.	CLC.	1923.	04.03.24.	10.1964.	01.12.66.
S93S.	7282.	TR.	CLC.	1923.	01.04.24.	10.1964.	01.12.66.
S94S.	7287.	TR.	CLC.	1923.	01.04.24.	10.1964.	05.01.67.
S95S.	7292.	TR.	CLC.	1923.	04.03.24.	10.1964.	16.02.67.
S96S.	7290.	TR.	CLC.	1923.	04.03.24.	10.1964.	08.07.66.

Types: DM: Driving Motor (A or D). CT: Control Trailer (A or D). TR: Trailer.

Standard Stock: Island Service Details.

No.	In Service.	Withdrawn.	To Mainland.	Disposal.
1	20.03.67.	06.06.90.	20.06.90.	07.01.93. Ruislip-VB (by road) scrap.
2	20.05.67.	07.09.90.	02.10.90.	LT Heritage Train Project.
3	20.03.67.	1989.	28.09.89.	04.10.90. Fratton-VB (by road) scrap.
4	20.03.67.	25.09.89.	28.09.89.	04.10.90. Fratton-VB (by road) scrap.
5	20.05.67.	13.05.91.		23.04.94. Scrapped Sandown. (GD).
6	15.05.67.	01.02.90.	14.03.90.	1991. Scrapped (BLM).
7	26.04.67.	07.09.90.	04.10.90.	LT Heritage Train Project.
8	22.03.67.	06.06.90.	22.06.90.	08.01.93. Ruislip-VB (by road) scrap.
9	26.04.67.	03.10.89.	13.03.90.	1991. Scrapped (BLM).
10	20.03.67.	06.06.90.	20.06.90.	05.01.93. Ruislip-VB (by road) scrap.
11	22.03.67.	18.01.90.	16.03.90.	15.01.93. Ruislip-VB (by road) scrap.
13	1967.	March 85.		June 87. Scrapped Ryde (RDC).
15	20.03.67.	07.10.67.		10.05.69. Scrapped at Ryde Depot.
15	1971.	11.04.88.		08.05.89. Scrapped Sandown (OT).
19	20.05.67.	12.1982.		21.04.89. Scrapped Sandown (OT).
20	1967.	11.04.88.		08.05.89. Scrapped Sandown (OT).
21	20.03.67.	03.1985.		06.1987. Scrapped Ryde (RDC).
22	20.03.67.	14.11.86.		16.05.89. Scrapped Sandown (OT).
23	15.05.67.	10.09.73.		04.05.74. Scrapped Ryde Depot.
25	22.03.67.	08.09.75.		10.1982. Scrapped Ryde Depot.
26	20.03.67.	07.09.90.		18.04.94. Scrapped Sandown (GD).
27	1967.	18.01.90.	03.10.90.	LT Heritage Train Project.
28	20.03.67.	13.05.91.		14.04.94. Scrapped Sandown (GD).
29	20.03.67.	25.09.89.	28.09.89.	16.10.90. Fratton-VB (by road) scrap.
30	20.05.67.	12.1982.		07.1987. Scrapped Ryde (RDC).
31	20.05.67.	13.05.91.		16.04.94. Scrapped Sandown (GD).
32	26.04.67.	04.09.89.	28.09.89.	15.10.90. Fratton-VB (by road) scrap.
33	20.03.67.	20.09.89.	26.09.89.	13.10.90. Fratton-VB (by road) scrap.
34	26.04.67.	06.06.90.	22.06.90.	20.10.90. Fratton-VB (by road) scrap.
36	22.03.67.	03.1985.		06.1987. Scrapped Ryde (RDC).
41	1967.	12.09.86.		08.05.89. Scrapped Sandown (OT).
42	20.03.67.	27.11.86.		16.05.89. Scrapped Sandown (OT).
43	20.05.67.	30.09.88.	05.07.89.	25.10.90. Fratton-VB (by road) scrap.
44	20.03.67.	03.02.90.	03.10.90.	LT Heritage Train Project.
45	15.05.67.	10.09.73.		04.05.74. Scrapped at Ryde Depot.
46	22.03.67.	14.02.86.		16.05.89. Scrapped Sandown (OT).
47	20.03.67.	11.1987.	05.07.89.	30.10.90. Fratton-VB (by road) scrap.
48	15.05.67.	10.09.73.		05.04.74. Scrapped Ryde Depot.
49	22.03.67.	07.09.90.	02.10.90.	LT Heritage Train Project.
92	20.03.67.	04.10.88.	26.09.89.	14.10.90. Fratton-VB (by road) scrap.
93	20.05.67.	18.01.90.	16.03.90.	20.10.90. Fratton-VB (by road) scrap.
94	26.04.67.	03.10.89.	13.03.90.	17.10.90. Fratton-VB (by road) scrap.
95	26.04.67.	05.03.90.	14.03.90.	23.10.90. Fratton-VB (by road) scrap.
96	22.03.67.	03.1985.		06.1987. Scrapped Ryde (RDC).

Note: BR car number S prefix & suffix omitted from this table for clarity. Breakers: BLM: Birds Long Marston. GD: Gwent Demolition of Margam. OT: Oxley Thomas. RDC: Ryde Demolition Co. VB: Vic Berry Leicestershire.

1967: Original Formations. (43 cars).

In Service.	Set.	Cars.		In Service.	Set.	Cars.			
20.03.67.	031	26	47	1	??.??.??.	041	20*	27	41	13
20.03.67.	032	28	92	3	20.03.67.	042	22*	29	42	15
20.05.67.	033	30	93	5	20.05.67.	043	2	31	43	19*
26.04.67.	034	32	94	7	20.03.67.	044	4	33	44	21*
26.04.67.	035	34	95	9	15.05.67.	045	6	48	45	23
22.03.67.	036	36	96	11	22.03.67.	046	8	49	46	25
					20.03.67.	Spare	10			

Builders.
CLC: Cammell Laird & Co. MCW: Metropolitan Carriage & Wagon Co. UCC: Union Construction & Finance Co, Feltham.

Bodies & Equipment.
The tube stock had timber body frames, with sheet steel external panels, mounted on steel under frames. The DM's were equipped with British Thomson-Houstan (BTH) electro-magnetic switchgear, resistances, compressors, and air reservoirs. The motor bogie had two GEC WT54A 240hp traction motors. Gear ratio 63:17. Maximum speed: 45 miles per hour.

Dimensions.
MCW Driving Motors: Length 51'5¼". Weight: 31 tons 15 cwt. Seating: 26.
*UCC Driving Motors: Length 49'9". Weight: 28 tons 19 cwt. Seating 26.
Control Trailers: Length 50'2½". Weight 17 tons 1 cwt. Seating 38.
Trailers: Length 49'9¼". Weight 18 tons 9 cwt. All cars: height 9'6". Width 8'8".

Typical train length and (seating).
3-car: 156'5½" (106). 4-car: 207'11" (132). 7-car: 364'4½" (238).

Control Trailers.
CT/A received yellow cab ends. CT/D were only used as trailers, with the cab ends painted blue. In 1983 the yellow ends were also painted blue, and all driving equipment was removed. Only S28S was used as a Control Trailer from 1987.

Liveries & Modifications.
Blue with grey doors: 39 cars painted from 28.01.76-13.05.80. 1-11/13/15/19-22/26-34/36/41-44/46-47/49/92-96.
Inter City blue & grey: 30 cars painted from 01.01.82-23.06.86. 1-2/5-10/15/20-22/26-29/31-34/41-47/49/92-94.
Network SouthEast: 24 cars from 07.02.87-15.05.89. 1-11/26-29/31-34/44/49/93-95.
Lime green Interiors: 33 cars from 14.02.81-13.11.87. 1-11/13/15/20/22/26-29/31-34/41-47/49/92-94. (Car 95 grey interior May 87).
Apple green interiors: 5 cars during April 1989. 1/9/31/32/94.
Cab front modifications: 14 cars from 06.06.85-29.06.88. 1-11/15/20/28.

Stock returned to the mainland.
A total of 23 cars returned to the mainland between 26.09.89-03.10.90, travelling from Sandown to Fratton, by road and ferry. The preserved stock left Fratton 18.10.90, under their own power to LT at Wimbledon, before moving on for storage. Cars 27 & 44 had been painted into LT red & cream at Ryde Depot. DM's 1/6-11 went by road from Fratton to LT for spares recovery before going for scrap. Challenge Films acquired DM's 6 & 9, for use in the movie 'Split Second', before they travelled by road for scrap. Apart from the preserved cars: 2/7/27/44/49 all of the Standard Stock used on the Island has been scrapped.

LT 1938 Stock (BR Class 483).

It had been planned that Standard Stock would be replaced after 10 years, but 21 years later 28 cars were still in service. In 1973 LT started to scrap 1938 Stock but BR decided not to buy any as it would be too vulnerable on Ryde Pier, because of under floor mounted equipment, and Ryde Depot would need expensive alterations. However, something had to be done, as closure had been discounted.

In April 1988 London Transport offered to sell BR 1938 stock, this time BR agreed to purchase 44 cars, but they decided not to use the trailers, which were subsequently scrapped. BR planned minimal preparation, as they intended to replace it with 1959/62 stock in 1995, but they decided on a higher specification refurbishment for a longer service life, and the 1959/62 stock was later scrapped.

It was not until August 1988 that Network SouthEast announced that they were going to bring the new trains to the Island, initially they planned to have ten, 2-car trains, but this was reduced to eight due to costs.

This shows how much travelling habits have changed, in 1967 42 cars were required for service, but in 1988 just 16 were adequate, and maximum train lengths were reduced from 7 to 4-cars. In fairness, a new 4-car train could carry an extra 36-seated passengers, when compared with the old 4-car trains.

The 1938 Stock was a bit of a trendsetter in its time, as it was the first Tube stock to have under floor mounted equipment, this allowed seating for 42, 16 more then the pre-38 power cars. During 1994-95 the seating in the A cars (except 125) was reduced to 40, to make room for a locker for the Guards equipment. 15.11.95.

The first four cars were transferred to British Rail Engineering Ltd (BREL) on November 11th 1988. Delivery of the remaining cars took place between February 3rd and September 12th 1989. The replacement trains, known as class 483, would usually run in 2-car formations, strengthened to 4-car trains during peak periods.

It was not until July 15th 1989 that the first two cars arrived on the Island, which were delivered to Sandown. The appropriately numbered 483001 travelled across the Solent on the Wightlink car ferry, from Portsmouth to Fishbourne. The pioneer car to be placed on Island rails was car 221 a D power car, once again the cars were designated A or D, with the A car still at the Ryde end.

Following testing the new train was introduced in a special ceremony held at Ryde Pier Head platform 2, on July 13th 1989, when the train was used to break a banner held across the line which read: "Network SouthEast welcomes new Isle of Wight trains". The train was then used on a shuttle service to Ryde Esplanade.

On September 26th 1989 unit 483002 arrived at Sandown, followed by 483003, the next day. On 01.10.89 the first trial run of a 4-car train was made, using 001/002. The next day a 6-car formation (001/002/003) made a trial run but it was decided that, under normal circumstances, 4-cars would be sufficient.

This photograph taken from Ryde signal box shows the newly arrived 002 propelling 003 into the depot. In the platform siding is 485044, with 485041 on No. 2 road, and the pioneer 483001 on No.4 road. The difference in the NSE livery used on Island trains can also be appreciated, with the revised colours on the class 483, with the colours swept up at the cab ends. On the mainland the original livery had the swept up ends, and the revised livery had the straight lines. Phil Evans.

It was not until March 1990 that further stock was delivered, when 007 arrived on the 12th, 004 on the 14th and 005 on the 15th. To accommodate the new trains, Ryde Depot was refurbished and number 1 road raised, so as to ease access to the under floor mounted equipment, and number 2 road gained a full length pit.

The depot was given an official re-opening, during those ceremonies, a plaque was unveiled; "This plaque was unveiled by Sir Robert Reid, Chairman of the British Railways Board, to commemorate the refurbishment of Ryde St. Johns Road Traction Maintenance Depot. Wednesday March 21st 1990".

Three months later two more trains were delivered, 006 on June 20th, followed by 008 the next day. Two years later NSE decided to send a further four cars to the Island, set 483010 arrived at Sandown on April 8th 1992, which were stripped out body shells, supplied as a reserve. 483009 arrived the next day; it entered traffic on June 18th, the whole fleet of 18 cars were now available for services.

483010 arrived on April 8th 1992, supplied as a strategic reserve it was nothing more then a stripped out shell, which stood for 6 years at the end of the down siding near the 1½-mile post, it was never required. In 1998 the bodies were lifted from their under frames, and placed in the car park at Ryde St. Johns. The two cars were scrapped in June, 7 years later, and the remains were taken to Clifton Grade's scrap yard at Somerton, on Thursday June 9th 2005. 01.06.97.

During the early hours of March 1st 1998 four other cars were lifted from the track, having been stripped of all usable parts. The bodies of 121 (nearest), 222, 223 and 125 are seen in the car park at Ryde St. Johns Road, where they were scrapped, Clifton Grade took the remains in April 2000. Cars 123 and 221 were not leased from HSBC Rail and are stored in the down siding, to the north of Ryde St. Johns station, weather beaten and liberally daubed in graffiti! 22.03.98.

483009 is seen in the yard, outside the depot, painted blue in prior to the application of the dinosaur livery. It is standing alongside the carriage cleaning platform, which came into use on July 17th 1990, cleaning had previously been carried out alongside the down platform. Also of interest is the electric capstan, which staff can use when they physically move un-powered stock. 21.02.00.

Once again dinosaurs roam the Isle of Wight! This is the moment that Island Line's radical new livery, devised by Alan Cracknell, was introduced to the media and invited guests. To the sound of Jeff Wayne's 'The Eve of the War', 483006 moves out of the depot, into bright sunshine. It was named Terry (short for Terri dactyl). It was no coincidence that this day was chosen for the launch, it was exactly 33 years since the electric era had started on the Island. 21.03.00.

Yet another new livery, this is 483007 in the early stages of its planned retro-look, the work had yet to be completed, but it looked quite superb sitting outside the depot. Unfortunately, it was not destined to remain so good-looking, it was attacked four times by graffiti vandals. Not only that, it was severely damaged during the 2000 floods, and for a time it seemed likely to be scrapped! 22.04.01.

It was not until January 24th 2003 that 007, 'licensed to thrill' was released to traffic. Island Line staff visited the LT Museum to ensure accuracy, which included LT logos and numbers being displayed. It was such a success that during October 2003, 483009 (seen at Ryde St. Johns) was painted into the same livery, but without the LT logos, so that a matching 4-car train can be formed. 18.12.03.

Class 483: Mainland Details.

Car.	LT No.	Delivered.	In Service.	From LT.	To BREL.	To Fratton.
121.	10184.	19.08.39.	01.09.39.	11.11.88/A.	12.11.88.	04.07.89.
221.	11184.	19.08.39.	01.09.39.	11.11.88/A.	12.11.88.	04.07.89.
122.	10221.	13.11.39.	09.12.39.	11.11.88/A.	12.11.88.	15.09.89.
222.	11221.	13.11.39.	09.12.39.	11.11.88/A.	12.11.88.	15.09.89.
123.	10116.	10.01.39.	23.01.39.	14.10.88.	03.02.89.	25.09.89.
223.	11116.	10.01.39.	23.01.39.	14.10.88.	03.02.89.	25.09.89.
124.	10205.	10.10.39.	04.11.39.	18.11.88.	07.04.89.	08.03.90#1
224.	11205.	10.10.39.	04.11.39.	18.11.88.	07.04.89.	08.03.90#2
125.	10142.	27.02.39.	05.05.39.	21.10.88.	14.04.89.	08.03.90#2
225.	11142.	27.02.39.	05.05.39.	21.10.88.	14.04.89.	08.03.90#1
126.	10297.	01.07.40.	21.02.42.	18.11.88.	28.04.89.	14.06.90#3
226.	11297.	01.07.40.	21.02.42.	18.11.88.	28.04.89.	14.06.90#3
127.	10291.	17.06.40.	18.10.40.	11.05.89/B.	19.05.89.	07.03.90#3
227.	11291.	17.06.40.	18.10.40.	11.05.89/B.	19.05.89.	07.03.90#3
128.	10255.	26.02.40.	31.05.40.	14.10.88.	26.05.89.	14.06.90#3
228.	11255.	26.02.40.	31.05.40.	14.10.88.	26.05.89.	14.06.90#3
129.	10229.	05.12.39.	19.01.40.	21.10.88.	12.09.89.	02.04.92.
229.	11229.	05.12.39.	19.01.40.	21.10.88.	12.09.89.	02.04.92.
130.	10139.	20.02.39.	15.03.39.	28.10.88.	#4.	01.04.92.
230.	11172.	13.07.39.	31.07.39.	28.10.88.	#4.	01.04.92.

Class 483: Island Details.

Car.	Arrived.	In Service.	Withdrawn.	Notes.
121.	05.07.89.	13.07.89.	28.06.96.	#5: 24.04.00. Scrapped at Ryde.
221.	05.07.89.	13.07.89.	16.05.95.	Off lease-stored at Ryde.
122.	26.09.89.	07.10.89.		
222.	26.09.89.	07.10.89.	20.06.96.	#5: 24.04.00. Scrapped at Ryde.
123.	27.09.89.	07.10.89.	16.05.95.	Off lease-stored at Ryde.
223.	27.09.89.	07.10.89.	16.12.94.	#5: 24.04.00. Scrapped at Ryde.
124.	13.03.90.	01.05.90.		
224.	13.03.90.	01.05.90.		
125.	15.03.90.	11.05.90.	16.12.94#6.	#5:24.04.00. Scrapped at Ryde.
225.	15.03.90.	11.05.90.		
126.	20.06.90.	13.07.90.		
226.	20.06.90.	13.07.90.		
127.	12.03.90.	18.05.90.		
227.	12.03.90.	18.05.90.		
128.	21.06.90.	29.06.90.		
228.	21.06.90.	29.06.90.		
129.	09.04.92.	18.06.92.		
229.	09.04.92.	18.06.92.		
130.	08.04.92.		01.03.98.	#5: Scrapped at Ryde by 09.06.05.
230.	08.04.92.		01.03.98.	#5: Scrapped at Ryde by 09.06.05.

Note: In some publications cars 130/230 are listed as 120/220.   Please see page 26 for further notes.

Original Formations.

Set.	A Car.	D Car.
483001	121	221
483002	122	222
483003	123	223
483004	124	224
483005	125	225
483006	126	226
483007	127	227
483008	128	228
483009	129	229
483010	130	230

2005 Formations.

Set.	A Car.	D Car.
483002	122	225
483004	124	224
483006	126	226
483007	127	227
483008	128	228
483009	129	229

Formation Changes.

29.06.90: 003: 123+224, 004: 124+223. **21.10.91:** 003: 123+223. **31.10.91:** 004 124+224. **04.01.94:** 009 129+224 (due to flood damage). **08.02.94:** 004 124+224. 009: 129+009. 10.02.94: 003: 123+225. 005: 125+223. **16.05.95:** 001: 121+225. 003: 123+221. **28.06.96:** 001: 121+222. 002: 122+225.

Modifications & Livery Changes (ex-Network SouthEast).

Set.	Locker.	Tripcock.	Painted.	Livery.	Name.	Repainted.	Livery.
002	30.11.94.	17.04.02.	20.04.00.	DN.	Raptor.		
003.	17.12.94.						
004.	24.11.94.	12.01.02.	21.03.00	DN.	Terry.		
006.	06.02.95.	01.01.02.	20.03.00.	DN.	T-Rex.		
007.	16.03.95.	24.01.03.	24.01.03.	LT1.			
008.	09.03.95.	02.02.02.	24.07.00.	DN.	Iggy.		
009	24.03.95.	03.02.02.	10.03.00.	DN.	Bronti.	October 03.	LT2.

Notes.

All stock handed over at Ruislip, then transferred to Strawberry Hill except: A: Went direct to BREL via Clapham. B: From White City to BREL via Wimbledon. #1&2: ran as pairs until transfer to the Island, when they resumed correct formations. #3: Due to extension of Underground services over lines owned by the LNER, ownership of 289 cars (including these six) passed to the LNER, although they were operated and maintained by LT. In 1948 ownership passed back to LT, with the formation of the British Transport Commission (BTC). #4: Date to British Rail Engineering Ltd, Eastleigh (BREL) not known, supplied as strategic reserve. #5: February 28th/March 1st 1998 the bodies were lifted from the rails at Ryde St. Johns Road. #6: 10.02.94. Car 125 collided with the buffers at Ryde Pier Head.

Livery notes: DN: Blue with Dinosaur decals. LT1: London Transport 1930's livery red bodywork, with cream window pillars. Grey roof, black underframes and mandatory yellow warning panel. London Transport branding and decals. LT2: Livery as LT1 but without the London Transport branding and decals.

Technical Details.

Built by Metropolitan-Cammell, Saltley. From an order placed by LT for 624 DM's.
A Car: Seating 40 (originally for 42 until Guards locker replaced two seats). BR Lot number: 31071. Diagram: EA265. Equipment: 2xcollectors shoes. 2x168hp traction motors. Motor Generator set. 50volt battery. Inverter.
D Car: Seating 42. BR Lot number: 31072. Diagram: EA266. Equipment: 2xcollector shoes. 2x168hp traction motors. Compressor.

CHAPTER 3

RYDE TRAIN CARE DEPOT (RY)

This is how the Depot looked, before refurbishment in 1989. 486031 is on number 2 road, with an unidentified Control Trailer (D) on number 4 road, it has been used as a trailer as the cab end is painted black. The body of former Control Trailer (A) S30 is on the right, being used as a store. It had been withdrawn from 486033 in 1982, and was eventually scrapped in July 1987, at Ryde Depot. Phil Evans.

The main building was built in 1938, for carriage & wagon repairs, replacing an earlier IWR structure. Ryde Shed came under Eastleigh district and was coded 71F by BR, but on transfer to Nine Elms area it became 70H, and in 1967 it became RY. When Newport shed (70G) closed in 1957, Ryde became responsible for 21 locomotives, 2 class E1 0-6-0 and 19 class 02 0-4-4-tank locos. 21.04.97.

Number 1 road was raised during 1989-90, to ease maintenance on the under floor mounted equipment. For obvious safety reasons the line is not electrified, power is fed from an overhead supply by an umbilical cord, the red light above the train shows that the power is on. The sign at the top of the steps reads: "When we do it right no one remembers, when we do it wrong no one forgets". 06.02.96.

Ryde staff can undertake most of the maintenance on their aging stock, although traction motors are usually sent to the mainland. Four hydraulic jacks have lifted the body of car 227, so that the bogies can receive attention. During major refurbishment, the traction motors are sent to REW, the engineering section of London Underground, at Acton. There is very close co-operation between REW and Island Line, which has cured many a problem, over the years. Kevin Weeks.

The building dates from 1938, the same year as the stock, but the work area is clean and bright, as befits Health & Safety requirements. The staff have removed these bogies, which were sent to Acton for overhaul. It is expensive maintaining such elderly stock, which is where REW can help, with standard items such as wheels. Depot staff, led by Jess Harper, really do perform miracles! 05.12.97.

Number 3 road is in an area known as the 'Turnery', which had originally been a two-road engine shed. In 1873 the IWR built a new loco shed, which allowed this building to be incorporated into the Carriage & Wagon Works. Car 225 has been masked and primed, prior to the application of Dinosaur livery. 21.03.00.

CHAPTER 4

TRACK MAINTENANCE. LOCOMOTIVES

Since 1966 three shunters have been used on Island Line, all have now left the route. This was the first, a 30-ton Hunslet 0-6-0 (later class 05), which arrived 07.06.66. Built in 1955 the cab roof was lowered at Eastleigh, to fit the restricted Island clearances. It has carried several numbers 11140, D2554, 2554, 05001 and 97803. It was in BR green on arrival, but was painted BR Blue in 1972, in 1984 it was sold to Haven Street where it regained Green livery in 1987. 15.02.98.

Built at Doncaster in 1960 this Class 03, 30-ton 0-6-0 arrived 08.04.84, and had its cab lowered at Ryde Depot. It too has carried several numbers, D2079, 2079 and 03079; it was to have become 97805 but retained its 03 number. After a long period out of use, it was withdrawn 06.06.96, and stored at Sandown. 30.06.96.

Built at Swindon in 1962 as D2179, it was renumbered 2179 and then 03179. It was withdrawn at Ipswich in July 1987, and is seen arriving at Ryde on 30.06.88. Prior to entering traffic its cab roof was lowered, and it was repainted in NSE livery, but it was withdrawn in October 1993. 236 class 03's were built between 1957-62, they have a Gardner 8L3 204hp engine, with 3'7" wheels. Phil Evans.

This poignant view shows the two classmates at Sandown, on their last day on the Island. Both had been sold and left the next morning, 03079 went to the Derwent Valley Railway near York. West Anglia Great Northern Railway (WAGN) purchased 03179, for use at their Hornsey Depot. This is the only class 03 to get full NSE livery, and the last working example on the National Rail Network. 04.06.98.

On May 6th 1967 two 15-ton brake vans, DS55710 & DS55724 (pictured) arrived, to assist with the electrification programme. Both were built in 1934 at Ashford, for the Southern Railway, part of a batch of just 50 examples. The former was sold to Haven Street in January 1985 and this one, painted in grey/yellow known as 'Dutch' livery (albeit rather weathered), followed in July 2000. 04.04.96.

DS7000 Britannia is a rail-lifting wagon, which is mounted on a 38'8" under frame that dates from 1935. It had originally been 58' in length, and had been used on a LSWR passenger carriage, which was scrapped in 1957. It was shortened to this length and used on a track-relaying unit until 1976, when it was stored until 1982. It was refurbished and equipped with 2 Geismar cranes and lighting, as most work was done at night, before arriving at Sandown on August 17th 1982. 04.04.96.

Britannia was semi-permanently coupled to two 13-ton Lowfit wagons, coded ZDP. DB453255 (pictured) and DB452219 were both built at Shildon, the former in 1959 the latter in 1957. The sides and ends were removed, and lighting fitted, in preparation for their new role, at Ramsgate Wagon Depot in 1980. Following a period of storage they arrived 17.08.82, being delivered to Sandown. 04.04.96.

On 09.07.86 two 13-ton Medfit wagons DB460239/DB461225 (pictured) arrived, both had been built at Ashford the former in 1952, the latter in 1956. They were overhauled at New Cross Gate, prior to transfer to the Island. They have full length drop sides and were used for general loads, such as dirty ballast or sleepers. 'For use on Isle of Wight only' is painted on the middle panel. 26.05.97.

On August 17th 1982 two 25-ton four wheeled Lowmac wagons arrived, coded ZVV. DE263276 and DE263289 were both built at Darlington in 1945, for the London & North Eastern Railway (LNER). The low main deck made for easier loading/unloading of sleepers; they were painted in 'Dutch' grey/yellow. 04.04.96.

Built for the Great Western Railway (GWR) at Swindon in 1944 as 100715 and later W100715, it was subsequently renumbered DW100715, prior to arriving on the Island July 9th 1986. When it first arrived it was fitted with planked sides, but these were later removed to ease loading/unloading of sleepers. This wagon coded ZRV, also carried a portable generator to power tools and/or lighting. 09.04.96.

In September 1989 three Dogfish ballast wagons arrived at Sandown, DB992739 (nearest) on the 26th, followed two days later by DB983247 (pictured) and DB993598, they were built in 1960/1956/1960. They have 3 hopper doors 8'7½" long; each chute is controlled by one of the white painted wheels. They have a wheelbase of 14 feet, and are 22'6" in length (over the buffers). 04.04.96.

On 08.04.92, two match wagons ADB452604/ADB453241 arrived at Sandown. Built in 1957/1959 as 13 ton Lowfits, they were converted in 1978 with conventional draw gear at one end, and tube stock couplings at the other, for Waterloo & City stock. ADB453241 is positioned between 03179 and 483010, demonstrating how movements would be made. At the time of writing the two match wagons and ballast wagon DB993598 are the only hauled stock left on the route (all long since withdrawn), the rest went to Haven Street in 2000. 02.02.96.

Instead of keeping expensive conventional stock idle for long periods, Road/Rail equipment is moved in, as and when required. This Fiat/Hitachi has been used to clear weeds from the Engineers siding, at Sandown, but it can also assist with ballasting, construction and trimming line side vegetation. 12.07.00.

The two Permaquip Personnel Carriers can each carry 9 staff (with full messing facilities) to the work site, towing the small trailer at speeds of up to 40 mph. These versatile units have an integral turntable, which allows the cab to always face the direction of travel. 68810 (nicknamed LaLa) arrived in November 1995, it was used on de-icing duties, but trains 004 and 009 now do this work. 68809 arrived two years later but it was sold to Haven Street in January 2005. 18.06.00.

CHAPTER 5

THE ROUTE DESCRIBED

The distances are expressed in Miles and Chains (M: Ch).
(1 chain = 22 yards. 80 chains = 1 mile).

M: Ch.		M: Ch.	
0:00	**Ryde Pier Head station.**	4:18½	Vicarage Lane (FPX).
0:32	**Ryde Esplanade station.**	4:33	Wall Lane Bridge (23) [O].
0:36	Signal WFP34 (L) [D].	4:46	Jones (FPX).
0:36	Signal WFP 35(L) [D].	**4:55**	**Brading station.**
0:38½	Footbridge. (2A) [O].	4:58	Cattle creep (26) [B].
0:43	Pump house.	4:59	Barnes (FPX).
0:44	Tunnel: London End. (3).	5:07	Yarbridge. (27) [O].
0:62	Tunnel: Country End. (3).	5:15	Brewhouse (OCX).
0:66	Signal: Fixed distant. (S) [D].	5:34	Thomas (OCX).
0:75	Rink Road Bridge. (4) [O].	5:47	Lower Morton (OCX).
1:02	Park Road Bridge. (5) [O].	5:55	Morton cattle creep.
1:07½	Signal WFP 30 (S) [D].	5:65	River Bridge (31) [B].
1:13	Signal WFP 14 (L) [U].	5:70	Road Bridge. (32) [B].
1:15	St. Johns Road Bridge (6) [O].	5:77	Farm Bridge. (33) [B].
1:19	**St. Johns Road station.**	6:01	Sandown power station.
1:20	Platform footbridge. (8) [O].	6:11¼	Signal WFP AR (L) [D].
1:21¾	Signal WFP 29 (S) [D].	6:15	Gills footbridge. (34) [O].
1:22	St. Johns Road signal box (WFP).	6:38¾	Signal WFP 51 (L) [U].
1:39	Signal WFP 15 (S) [U].	**6:42**	**Sandown station.**
1:52½	Signal: Fixed distant. (S) [U].	6:44½	Signal WFP 50 (L) [D].
1:60¼	Pig Leg (FPX).	6:46	Cox's subway [B].
1:69½	Signal WFP 28R (L) [D].	6:66½	Drabbles (FPX).
1:78	Pennyfeathers Bridge (12) [O].	6:79½	Signal WFP BR (L) [U].
1:79¼	Signal WA 455 (L) [U].	7:00	Lake Girder Bridge (36) [B].
2:05¼	Signal WFP 28 (L) [D].	7:19	Lake subway (37) [B].
2:09	Signal WA 455R (L) [U].	**7:24¼**	**Lake station.**
2:16¾	**Smallbrook Junction station.**	7:43	Cliff top (FPX).
3:12	Truckells Bridge (18) [O].	7:49	Skew footbridge (37A) [O].
3:49¼	Rowborough power station.	7:49	Skew Road Bridge (38) [O].
3:30	Rowborough Bridge (20) [O].	7:70	Footbridge (38A) [O].
3:76	Cattle creep (21) [B].	**8:29**	**Shanklin station.**
		8:31	End of the Line.

Throughout this section, on current track plans, signals are shown as:

‾‾‾‾‾| **Semaphore.**   —∞ **2-aspect colour light.**

Notes: Direction: [U] Up towards Ryde. [D] Down towards Shanklin.
Signals: (S) Semaphore. (L) Colour Light (All 2-aspect).
Bridges: [B] Below the line. [O] Over the line.
Structures: A number in brackets refers to the structure number, e.g. (2A).
Crossings: (FPX) Footpath crossing. (OCX): Occupation crossing, which maintains a right of way between fields (or property) separated by the railway.

IWR STATION LAYOUTS: CIRCA 1865.

Ryde St. Johns Road.

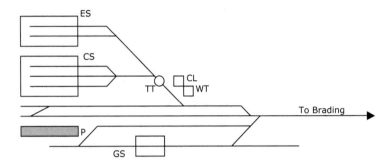

Brading.
(3 miles 36 chains from Ryde St. Johns Road).

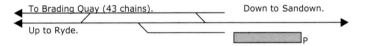

Sandown.
(5 miles 30 chains from St. Johns Road).

Shanklin.
(7 miles 9 chains from Ryde St. Johns Road).

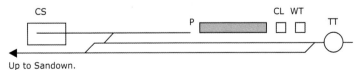

KEY:
CL: Coal stage. CS: Carriage shed. ES: Engine shed. GS: Goods shed.
P: Platform (all 200ft). TT: Turntable. WT: Water tank.

RYDE PIER HEAD

Pre-1933.

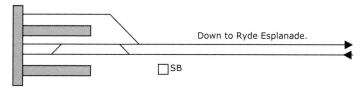

Down to Ryde Esplanade.

SB

1933-1966.

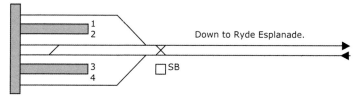

Down to Ryde Esplanade.

SB

1967-1973.

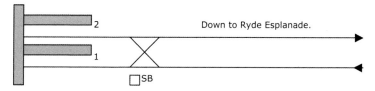

Down to Ryde Esplanade.

SB

1974-Today.

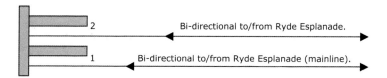

Bi-directional to/from Ryde Esplanade.

Bi-directional to/from Ryde Esplanade (mainline).

KEY:
SB: Signal Box.
1-4: Platform numbers.
Using the 1966 diagram platforms 1-3: 388 feet. Platform 4: 362 feet.

Ryde Pier Head station opened on July 12th 1880, having been constructed for the joint LSWR/LBSCR, the IWR ran the first train into the station. Originally comprising 3 roads, it was enlarged to 4 roads by the Southern Railway in 1933, and then reduced to 2 during the winter of 1966-67. The offset canopy shows how the platform was extended across the former number 3 road. 02.05.97.

Nowadays most services use number 1 road, number 2 being retained for use during maintenance on the mainline. On this occasion 483006 is on 'Special duties', having conveyed guests from St. Johns Road, to introduce the Dinosaur livery. From left to Right: Graham Eccles (MD South West Trains). Alan Cracknell (Island Line Director). Brian Cox (former Stagecoach UK executive director). Steve Wade who succeeded Alan Cracknell as Chairman of Island Line. 21.03.00.

The support columns are all that remain of the former number 1 road, which was removed in 1966-67. At the start of the electric era around 2 million passengers were carried per year, requiring 7-car trains, with a peak five trains per hour. Nowadays there are around 1 million per year, with a peak requirement of just 3 trains per hour. Ryde Parish Church dominates the skyline as a 4-car train (483004/009) enters the station, at 10:42, reaching journeys end. 26.05.97.

There are three piers at Ryde; on the left is the original 1814 Promenade Pier. In the middle is the old tram pier, which was used from August 29th 1864 until January 26th 1969; one of the tramcars is preserved at the Bus Museum on Newport Quay. On a really hot summer's day 483008 arrives with a 4-car train at the Esplanade, with the 11:38 to Shanklin, on the 1880 built structure. 21.08.95.

32 CHAINS FROM RYDE PIER HEAD: JOURNEY TIME 3 MINUTES.

1966

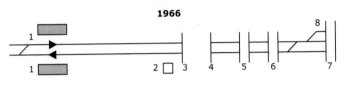

From 1973 (signals from 2000).

KEY:
1: Esplanade platforms (353'). 2: Pump House (43 chains). 3: Tunnel (London end 44 chains). 4: Tunnel (Country end 62 chains). 5: Rink Road Bridge (75 chains). 6: Park Road Bridge (1 mile 2 chains). 7: St. Johns Road Bridge (1 mile 15 chains). 8: Down loop (600'). 8A: Platform siding. 9: Trap point. 10: Footbridge (38 1/2 chains).

Signals & Signalling.
Signals: S1: WFP 34. S2: WFP 35. S3: Fixed Distant. S4: WFP 30. S5: WFP 14.
Note: S5 (WFP 14) was installed in March 2000, replacing WFP 14 (70 1/4 chains), and WFP 16 (1 mile 7 1/4 chains), the only 3-aspect signal on the route.
Ryde St. Johns Road signal box controls a mix of 2-aspect colour light signals, and three upper quadrant semaphore signals, in the Ryde area. Three types of train control are utilised. Track Circuit Block: Ryde Pier Head-Smallbrook. Tokenless Block: Smallbrook–Sandown. One-Train-In-Section: Sandown-Shanklin.

Direction of Travel.
Up.   Bi-directional.   Down.

Tunnels.

Location.	Length.	Company.
Ventnor (St. Boniface).	1,312 yards.	Isle of Wight Railway.
St. Lawrence (High Hat).	619 yards.	Newport, Godshill & St. Lawrence.
Ryde Esplanade.	391 yards.	Joint LSWR/LBSCR.
Cowes (Mill Hill).	208 yards.	Cowes & Newport Railway.
Newport.	73 yards.	Ryde & Newport Railway.

On the London end portal of Ryde tunnel is a block, which incorrectly commemorates the building of the tunnel in 1881, instead of 1880.

The station opened on April 5th 1880, built on a 9 chain left curve, the 353' platforms are connected by subway. Unusually, 483008 is using the former down line, due to maintenance on number 1 road. Ahead of the train is a trap point which is interlocked with the signal. If a train passes a red light it will be de-railed, so as to avoid any possibility of a collision. In May 1995 this was the first station to get the post BR house colours of Oxford blue and magnolia. 15.03.00.

483009 leads a 4-car train out of Ryde tunnel up the 1 in 50 gradient to reach the Esplanade, at the end of the 1³/₄-mile double track from Smallbrook. The tunnel clearance is just 12'3¹/₂", compared with 13'1" on the mainland, one of the main reasons why ex-Tube stock had to be used. Work on a new Esplanade transport interchange, costing £5.5 million, is due to start in the autumn of 2005. 28.10.95.

With a light dusting of snow on the track, 002 emerges from Rink Road Bridge (4) at 75 chains, on a 10 chain right curve. On the left is the site of the former Gas Works, which was rail served until 1955, there had been a trailing point from the up line by the bridge. As there was no connection to the down line, up to 15 coal wagons had to be propelled wrong-line back to St. Johns Road station. 08.02.96.

The line continues under Park Road Bridge (5) at 1 mile 2 chains, before sweeping round a 16-chain left curve, under St. John Road Bridge (6). Engineers can be seen installing a new up signal (WFP 14) and a train stop device, known as a Trip Cock, which will prevent a train passing the signal when a red light is displayed. In the down siding are cars 123/221, which are stored off-lease. 21.03.00.

1 MILE 19 CHAINS FROM RYDE PIER HEAD: JOURNEY TIME 6 MINUTES.

1966

1
2
3
4
Down carriage siding.
5
6
7
339'   420'
8
9
9 SB
SJ   10
ES
12   15
13   16
14   17

Present.

18
RD
Down siding 759'.
Down Platform siding.
9 S1
9 SB
SJ   S2   S3

KEY:
ES: Engine Shed. RD: Ryde Depot. SB: Signal Box. SJ: St Johns Road Bridge.
Signals: S1: WFP 29. S2: WFP 15. S3: Fixed Distant.
1: Engine Repair. 2: Carriage bogie repairs. 3: Carriage Lifting road. 4: Machine Shop (Turnery). 5-7: Carriage & Wagon Works. 8: Down loop (600ft). 9: Platforms (341ft) with footbridge. 10: Stores Road (240ft). 11: No. 4 Loco Road. 12: No. 3 Loco Road. 13: No. 2 Loco Road. 14: No. 1 Loco Road. 15: No.2 up siding (400ft). 16: No. 3 up siding (470'). 17: No. 4 up siding (600'). 18: Cleaning platform.

Ryde St Johns was the original IWR northern terminus; it had a 200-foot platform, on the up side of the line, with an engine run around loop. There was a 2-road brick built engine shed and a wooden, 3-road carriage shed, on the down side of the line. In 1866 a second platform was added, to the down side of the loop, in time for the opening of the Shanklin to Ventnor extension.

During 1871 the Ryde Pier Company (RPC) extended their standard gauge tramway to the station, which required a level crossing on St. Johns Road, for the first time IWR wagons could be horse drawn to and from the pier. During 1873 a new and larger engine shed was built on the up side of the line.

In June 1875 a new line was built, parallel with the existing IWR track, south to Smallbrook. The station was enlarged and a signal box was built at the south end of the up platform this, and the associated signalling etc, cost over £1,000 (shared by both companies). The work was carried out in preparation for the Ryde & Newport Railway service to Newport, which started on December 20th 1875. From that date IWR services used the down platform, while IWC used the up platform.

In 1879 the down platform was enlarged and a footbridge was provided to link both platforms, and a road bridge replaced the level crossing. This work was carried out for the opening of the new double track section, provided by the LSWR/LBSCR Joint Railway Companies, which opened to traffic in 1880.

The Southern Railway invested heavily at St. Johns Road, including a new 2-road loco shed during May 1930, which could accommodate eight tank locomotives. During 1938 the Carriage & Wagon Shop was replaced, and it is this structure that forms the present Depot. The track layout was reduced to its present size, on February 2nd 1975, when the final connection to the up sidings was lifted.

The up platform is on the site of the original 200' platform, the down platform was added in 1866 and, over the years, both have been extended to 341'. During May 1997 the station was repainted into the new house colours of blue and magnolia. This shade of blue provides a tenuous link with the IWR, as some of their stock carried a heraldic garter, whose body colour was Oxford blue. 01.07.00.

The first platform footbridge was installed during October 1879, in readiness for the opening to Ryde Pier. This new structure, at 1 mile 20 chains replaced one at the north end of the platforms in March 2000, as part of a £300,000 station re-generation programme. During July 2005 the car park was enlarged by 110 spaces, for the increasingly popular, Island Line Park & Ride scheme. The Park & Ride is also available from Brading, Sandown and Shanklin Stations. 21.03.00.

Ryde Signal Box (1 mile 22 chains), or Island Line Signalling Centre, as it is now known! This ex-South East & Chatham Railway (SECR) box stood at Waterloo Junction until being moved here in 1926, it is the only operational signal box on the 8½-mile route, at one time there had been eight! Ryde Esplanade closed in 1922, Ryde St. Johns Road North 1926, Smallbrook Junction 1966, Ryde Pier Head 1974, Shanklin 1979, Brading 1988 and Sandown on February 25th 1989. Brading box, although out of use, is the only other box still standing today. 25.04.96.

Apart from colour light signals, Ryde box controls three semaphore signals in the Ryde area, this is the up home (1mile 39 chains). Rounding a 35-chain left curve, on a rising gradient of 1 in 193, a 4-car train comprising 483008/004 head south. Standing in the down siding, 1/4-mile south of St. Johns Road is diesel shunter 03179, which was the last locomotive to be owned by Island Line. 26.05.97.

At 2miles 5¹/₄ chains signal WFP 28 protects the entrance to the single line section, south to Brading. If a train passes a red signal, which is known as a SPAD (signal passed at danger), the train will be diverted into a sand drag, in order to avoid the possibility of a collision. This view of Smallbrook Junction was taken from Pennyfeathers Bridge (12) at 1 mile 78 chains, using a telephoto lens. 02.05.97.

2 MILES 16³/₄ CHAINS FROM RYDE PIER HEAD. JOURNEY TIME: 9 MINUTES.

1926-1966

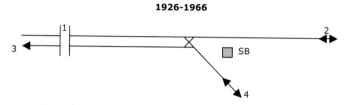

Note: The junction was 2 miles 10 chains from Ryde Pier Head.

1967-1991.

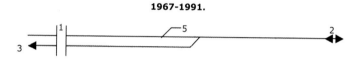

From 1991.

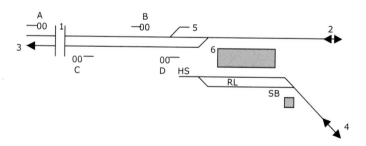

KEY:
Signals: A: WFP 28R. B: WFP 28. C: WA 455. D: WA 455R. A & D have the suffix letter R to indicate that they are repeater signals for B & C.
1: Pennyfeathers Bridge (12) 1 mile 78 chains.
2: To/from Brading 2 miles 37 chains.
3: To St. Johns Road 77_ chains.
4: To/from Haven Street 4 miles 18 chains.
5: Catch point & sand drag.
6: Smallbrook Junction station.
HS: Headshunt. RL: Run round loop. SB: Signal Box.

From 1875 the IWR and the RNR lines went their separate ways, with no connection between the lines. The Southern Railway opened the junction on 18.07.1926, which by the 1960's was reckoned to be the busiest single line junction in Britain, with 12 trains per hour on peak Summer Saturdays. On July 20th 1991 Mr Chris Green, of Network SouthEast opened the station. 29.05.01.

This Station is only open when the Steam Railway is operating, providing a cross-platform connection, with a journey into history. The preserved railway facilities include a run round loop, which 24 Calbourne is using, to get to the front of the train, for the return trip to Haven Street. The two white discs above the buffers, indicate the route code for a Cowes train, introduced by the Southern. 27.08.95.

South of Smallbrook the line continues to climb until just after the 3-mile post, where it starts to descend. Deep in Whitefield's Wood, hemmed in by the lush undergrowth, 483008 has just rounded a 50-chain left curve to reach the summit of that climb. On either side of the track can be seen a white diamond shape mounted on a post, which indicates to the driver that he can shut off the power, and coast down the gradient. This view is from Truckells Bridge (18). 02.05.97.

483007/003 lean to a 16 chain right curve, as they clear Wall Lane Bridge (23), at 4 miles 33 chains. In the steam era the speed limit was 40 mph, the electric trains are allowed to do a maximum of 45 mph. Records show that, on occasions, drivers did go a little faster! During 1931 the 06:30 from Ventnor to Ryde Pier Head, behind Adams 02 locomotive No. 21 Sandown, clocked up an incredible 56¹/₂ mph passing Smallbrook Junction! The 12¹/₂-mile journey took 28 minutes 6 seconds, against a normal time of around 43 minutes. [Railways in the Wight]. 08.12.95.

4 MILES 55 CHAINS FROM RYDE PIER HEAD. JOURNEY TIME: 14 MINUTES.

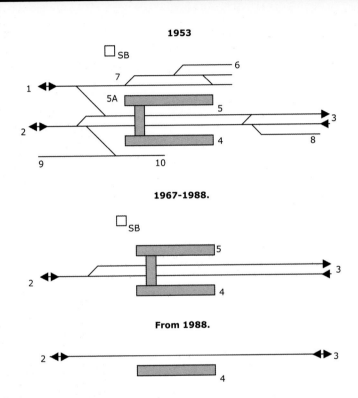

1953

1967-1988.

From 1988.

KEY:
SB: Signal Box. 1: To/From St. Helens & Bembridge. 2: To/From Smallbrook.
3: To/From Sandown. 4:Up platform 329' (showing footbridge). 5: Down platform 334'. 5A: Branch platform 211'.
6: Siding 80'. 7: Loop 100'. 8: Chalk siding 720'. 9: Siding 60'. 10: Dock siding 185'.

Brading opened on August 23rd 1864, with a 200' platform on the up side of the line, 3 miles 36 chains from St. Johns Road. There was a single siding also on the up side, with a passing loop to the north of the platform, on the down side. From the loop was a ¹/₂-mile siding to Brading Quay, where there was a headshunt with a run round loop, on a wooden jetty.

The jetty was large enough to accommodate three 150-ton vessels; it was extended in 1871, when additional sidings were added. Brading Quay remained in use until the Bembridge branch was built, with a new harbour complex at St. Helens, which opened to traffic on August 1st 1878.

Opened on August 23rd 1864, Brading became an un-staffed halt in 1969, when Conductor Guards were introduced on the trains. The building was taken out of railway use and with a grant of £18,000 from British Rail; it was converted for use as Community Centre, which opened July 13th 1989. 12.07.00.

The down platform was added in 1870, when the passing loop was extended through the station. The station was further enlarged with the opening of the Bembridge branch in 1878, and in 1897 a footbridge was installed to link the two platforms. The last passenger train from Bembridge ran on Sunday 20th September 1953, although works train continued until November 1957. 24.10.95

Brading signal box opened in 1882, and was equipped with a 30-lever frame, although in the end only 5 levers were in use. This view was taken shortly before closure, on October 29th 1988; the track diagram shows the simplicity of the reduced layout. There were two block instruments, the one with the flat bell for the Smallbrook section, and the conical bell for the Sandown section. Phil Evans.

This was the view of the north end of the station, from the signal box, just prior to its closure. Waiting at the platform is set 485043, led by car S6, which dated from 1931. It had been in service with LT from February 1932-August 1966, and was in BR service from 15.05.1967-01.02.90. It returned to the mainland and featured in the film 'Split Second' before being scrapped in 1991. Phil Evans.

This north facing view was taken from Barnes footpath crossing at 4 miles 59 chains, and shows how the down platform and signal box although out of use, are still extent. The grey house on the left had been the Station Masters house, which was built in 1877, but is now a private residence. As Brading is midway on the route, Stagecoach would like to re-instate the passing loop, so that a 30-minute service can replace the present irregular 20 and 40-minute intervals. 04.05.98.

On this section (near the 5 mile post) the line is just a couple of feet above sea level, and is hemmed in by Brading Down to the west, and the eastern River Yar. 483009 speeds south towards Yarbridge (27) at 5 miles 7 chains, it will then pass occupation crossings at Brewhouse (5 miles 15 chains) and Thomas (5 miles 34 chains). Remnants of melting snow can be seen on the riverbank. 08.02.96.

A southbound service descends Morton Bank, with the blue waters of Sandown Bay in the distance, and the River Yar meandering close to the line. The sea used to enter the low laying land between the railway and the Bay, until 1388 when Sir William Russell of Yaverland had a causeway constructed. The area was completely reclaimed when the BHR built the Bembridge branch in 1878. 20.05.96.

On a rising gradient of 1 in 77 the line climbs away from the Yar Valley, to pass beneath Gill's footbridge (34) at 6 miles 15 chains, before entering the passing loop. On 15.04.1871 two IWR trains collided in this cutting, but fortunately there was little damage and no one was seriously injured, thanks to prompt action by the drivers. The southbound train was a 'Special' conveying the IWR Chairman and invited guests from the LSWR, on a tour of the route! 28.02.96.

6 MILES 42 CHAINS FROM RYDE PIER HEAD. JOURNEY TIME: 19 MINUTES.

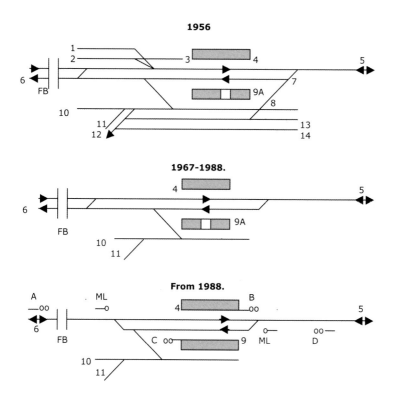

KEY:
FB: Gills Footbridge. 1: No. 7 Road 380'. 2: Straight Road 360'. 3: Dock siding 100'. 4: Down platform 396'. 5: To/from Shanklin. 6: To/from Brading.
7: Passing loop 725'. 8: Inner loop 384'. 9: Up platform 396'. (9A: with signal box). 10: Brickfields siding 160'.
11: Ditches siding 360'. 12: To/from Merstone (5 miles 64 chains). 13: Middle siding 120'. 14: Outside siding 360'.
Signals: A: WFP AR. B: WFP 50. C: WFP 51. D: WFP BR. ML: Marker Light.

From 1988: The passing loop points are train activated, they are set for arrivals, departing trains physically push the blades over, which reset after approximately 10 seconds. A marker light (ML) informs the driver that the point is correctly set, if the light is extinguished the driver must stop the train and investigate. The driver would inform Ryde signal box and, if necessary, manually reset the points.

The station opened on August 23rd 1864, 5 miles 21 chains from Ryde St. Johns Road. There was a single wooden platform, on the down side of the line, with a two-storey building. A passing loop was laid just to the north, which was extended through the station in 1866, and a platform was added to the up side of the loop.

During 1869 the down platform building was enlarged to incorporate the head office for the IWR. During the following year extra sidings were laid, on the up side of the station, in readiness for cross-country line to Merstone and Newport.

In 1874 the up platform was extended and a wooden footbridge was installed, at the north end of the platforms. A connection was laid from the IWR lines to those used by the Newport Junction Railway, which was controlled by a new signal box, which was built at the north end of the up platform. These works cost just over £438, which was shared between the two companies.

A subway (structure 35) replaced the footbridge in 1893, when the up platform was enlarged, and at the same time a new waiting room was built. A replacement elevated signal box was built over the waiting room, which was equipped with a 32-lever Saxby & Farmer frame, which led to the demolition of the 1874 box.

The Southern Railway lengthened both platforms in 1939, to their present dimensions, so as to accommodate 6-carriage trains. In 1956 the Newport line closed, and in 1966-67 the station was further rationalised in readiness for the electric era, including the lifting of all the sidings on the down side of the line.

In 1975 the footpath level crossing, just south of the platforms was replaced by a new subway, which cost in the region of £14,500. At 6 miles 46 chains from Ryde Pier Head, this replacement feature is known as Cox's subway.

Sandown station, basking in warm autumnal sunshine, was the IWR headquarters for many years; Island Line also had their offices here until January 1997, when they were relocated to Ryde St. Johns Road station. On December 14th 2003 a new buffet opened in the main building, and from Tuesday 4th May 2004 Optio started route 104 (Sandown station-Brading via Yaverland), using this 'Wave Bus' branded Optare Alero low floor minibus (HW04 DDJ). The bus service was not successful and came to an end on Friday 22nd July 2005, with the loss of 5 jobs. 18.10.04.

Early 1989 and time is running out for Sandown's lofty signal box, by this time the box was 96 years old, and the combined age of 4-car set 485044 was 248 years! Driving Motor (D) 7 was painted in NSE livery during February 1988, and was withdrawn in September 1990, one month later it was returned to the mainland. It has been retained for London Transport's Heritage Train project. Phil Evans.

On a bright crisp winter's afternoon, 008 and 007 pass at Sandown, as passenger trains have been doing since 1866, when the loop was extended through the station. Close examination between the rails in the foreground, will reveal the roof panels of the subway (No. 35), which opened in 1893. On May 14th 2005 a new entrance was opened which gives direct access to the up platform for passengers, and the large number of pupils, who attend the nearby schools. 21.02.04.

This was the view from Sandown signal box, looking south, on the far right is the former Driving Motor (D) S19, which had been withdrawn from set 043 in 1982. It arrived here in March 1984, having been renumbered 083569 in the Internal User series, for use as a store until it was scrapped in 1989. The reformed 043 faces a 19-chain left curve and a climb of 1 in 80, as it leaves for Shanklin. Phil Evans.

Leaving Sandown trains face a stiff climb of 1 in 80 through Los Altos Park, where they pass Drabbles footpath crossing, at 6 miles 66$^{1}/_{2}$ chains. The gradient eases at Lake Girder Bridge (7 miles), which takes the line over the A3055. The road was lowered in January 1972, to give clearance of 15'9", to allow modern high-sided vehicles, including double deck buses at 13'8" to pass beneath. 24.10.95.

7 MILES 24¼ CHAINS FROM RYDE PIER HEAD, JOURNEY TIME 21 MINUTES.

The wooden platform was built on the down side of the line, at a cost of £80,000, and was opened on July 9th 1987. It is provided with a simple shelter, CCTV and a help/emergency link to Ryde signal box (as are all stations on the route). This shelter was on site from 1996-2004, when a new one was installed at a cost of £5,000, which was jointly funded by Lake Community Partnership. 17.05.98.

483006 can be seen leaving the station, on an 80-chain right curve, on a rising gradient of 1 in 118. In the foreground is the 7½ mile post, these distance markers are sited every ¼-mile, each black line beneath the number represents one quarter of a mile. The IWR directors requested mileposts and gradient markers to be installed in May 1864, 3 months before the line opened. 02.05.97.

A long sweeping right curve of 80 chains, on a rising gradient of 1 in 118, is faced south of Lake. Trains pass Cliff top footpath crossing (7 miles 43 chains), before reaching Lake Skew Bridge (38) at 7 miles 49 chains, which is the fourth and final time that the A 3055 and the railway cross each other. In the early 1900's there had been two fields between the railway and the crumbling cliff edge. 01.08.99.

From Skew Bridge the line passes the County Cricket Ground, and on the left is the site of Lake Halt, which opened on Monday August 19th 1889, in time for a visit by HRH Prince Henry of Battenburg, for a cricket match. The platform cost just over £14, but it only remained in use for 25 years, and was closed in 1914. This view was taken from Alresford Road footbridge (38A) at 7 miles 70 chains, which was opened in 1969, replacing an earlier footpath crossing. 05.06.96.

8 MILES 29 CHAINS FROM RYDE PIER HEAD. JOURNEY TIME: 24 MINUTES.

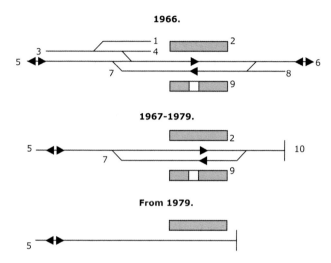

1966.

1967-1979.

From 1979.

KEY:
1: Back siding 440'. 2: Down platform 363'. 3: Headshunt 1,440'.
4: Dock siding 110'. 5: To/from Sandown. 6: To/from Wroxall (2 miles 55 chains).
7: Passing loop 462'. 8: Gas House siding 200'.
9: Up platform 379' with 20-lever signal box. 10: Headshunt (kick-back siding).

The Isle of Wight Railway had planned to reach Ventnor via Bonchurch, with Shanklin station at what is now known as the 'Old Village'. This coastal route would have required major engineering and earth works, and been extremely expensive. Local opposition was so great the IWR were forced to abandon their plans, and build an alternative route via Wroxall. The site of the present station was chosen in 1862, and was 7 miles 9 chains from Ryde St. Johns Road.

On Friday 19th August 1864 Colonel Yolland, on behalf of the Railway Department of the Board of Trade, inspected the Ryde-Shanklin route, and he recommended that the line could be opened. The first passenger train left Ryde at 06:00, on Tuesday 23rd August 1864, with just 12 passengers onboard.

The section south to Wroxall and Ventnor proved hugely expensive, and suffered from many delays. It was not until August 29th 1866 that the line was inspected, by Colonel Yolland, who deferred the opening until further works had been completed. The Colonel re-inspected the line in early September, and this time gave his approval for the section to open. The first passenger train left Ryde at 07:35, on Monday 10th September 1866, and took 25 minutes to reach Ventnor.

From August 1868 until 1876 the IWR were in the hands of an Official Receiver, and had to protect their rolling stock, and other assets, from creditors. With the help of the Receiver, Joseph Bourne, financial problems were solved and the IWR became the most successful of the three pre-grouping Island railway companies.

During 1880 the IWR carried 517,395 passengers and 53,543 tons of freight, providing an income of £32,623, with outgoings of £16,172.

The station was built on a 37-chain right curve, with a single platform on the down side of the line. The up platform was added in 1872, and was linked by a subway, there was a signal box with a 20-lever Saxby & Farmer frame on this platform from 1891-1979. In 1979 the former down platform was shortened at the south end, and extended at the north, the wider slabs show that extension. 15.04.97.

The end of the line is 8 miles 31 chains from Ryde Pier Head. From 1967 until 1969 both platforms were in use during peak periods, when there was a 5-train service, otherwise the up line was used for stock storage to ease the burden on Ryde St. Johns Road facilities. In July 1979 the signal box was closed, the loop was lifted, and the bridge over Landguard Manor Road demolished. 18.04.96.

The Shanklin-Ventnor section closed on April 18th 1966, thirty years later it was estimated that it would cost £10 million to re-open the line! In 1865, the first full year of operation over 252,855 passengers and 16,158 tons of freight were carried. During 1881, the first full year of Ryde Pier Head-Ventnor services, over 545,346 passengers and 52,187 tons of freight were carried. In 1922, the last full year of independence 1,217,925 passengers and 58,062 tons of freight were carried, nowadays there are around 1million passengers per year. 18.04.96.

From 1864, whilst the Shanklin-Ventnor section was constructed, Mews & Co met every train with two horse drawn buses, the service ended in 1866 when the line opened. When the line closed in April 1966 Southern Vectis route 39, linked the station to Ventnor, until May 1983. On Monday 04.10.04 Wight Bus started a new bus service between the two towns, using this dedicated Alexander Dennis Mini Pointer Dart (HW04 DCE), which is adorned with 'Rail Link' branding. 18.10.04.

Upper: 483002/004 leave St. Johns Road at 13:31 for Ryde Pier Head, standing outside the Depot are sets 005 and 007, both had their motors running to prevent them freezing. *Lower:* At 13:28, 483009 accelerates south towards Smallbrook, on a 35 chain left curve, towards an unidentified train standing in the down siding.

Island Line is subject to a strict performance regime. Every cancellation, termination short of destination, and every train over 15 minutes late incurs a penalty fine of £100. The only exception being cancellations on Ryde Pier, due to heavy seas, which might damage under floor mounted electrical equipment.

Fortunately, being surrounded by water the Island weather is usually less extreme then on parts of the mainland there are, however, exceptions to every rule! These two views were taken from Ryde signal box, on February 6th 1996, after 4 inches of snow fell across the Island. Road transport suffered delays, and there were some minor accidents, Island Line services however were unaffected.

Above: *Serious flooding occurred 9/10th October 2000, causing an extensive washout of ballast, which is being inspected by Steve Wade. 11.10.00.* **Below:** *This dramatic view was taken inside Ryde Depot, as a torrent of floodwater rushed through the building, causing extensive damage to equipment and rolling stock. 09.10.00. Both views courtesy: Steve Wade/Island Line.*

In recent times it has been flooding that has caused most problems, as these views show. Exceptionally heavy rain fell on Christmas Eve 1999; around 21:00 Monkton Mead Brook burst its banks causing extensive damage, and stranding a 4-car train (002/008) at Shanklin, over the Christmas holiday.

On December 27th 009 recovered the errant train, and the 6 cars returned to Ryde, the longest passenger train for several years, although passengers were restricted to 009, (Trials for a 6-car train had been carried out on October 2nd 1989). Services were maintained by 009 for the rest of the day, using the down line, in both directions, until repairs were made that evening.

The torrential deluge, on October 9/10th 2000, flooded Ryde tunnel to a depth of eight feet! On the left is a pump house (at 43 chains), which usually prevents excessive disruption. In 1909 the original gas powered Crossley engine was replaced by electric motors, with a Lister standby engine. Courtesy: Steve Wade.

After the October 2000 flooding, trains were suspended for three days, with 230 services cancelled, and loss of revenue in the order of £10,000. Over 500 tonnes of ballast was required for washouts, some of which were 6 foot deep and 40 feet long. It was estimated that the total repair bill was in the region of £750,000!

Ryde Depot was flooded to a depth of 5 feet, which caused extensive damage to four trains, 002/004/006 and 007, which was so badly damaged it was thought it might have to be withdrawn. In the event 004 returned to traffic 13.10.00, 006 on 03.12.00, 002 on 20.06.01, and 007 on 24.01.03 with the launch of its LT livery.

Occasionally high tide, combined with rough seas, can cause the pier services to be suspended. When that occurs, it has prompted headlines such as "Wrong sort of tide halts train". Oh so predictable! But hey, no one said it was easy to operate trains on the Island, as two pre-grouping companies could testify.

On Friday March 4th 1870, the Cowes & Newport Railway took delivery of their third locomotive, a Black Hawthorn 0-4-2 saddle tank named *Mill Hill*. It was transported to the Island on a barge however, while being unloaded it fell over the side, to land in the River Medina. It was eventually salvaged and entered service, non-the worse for its adventure; it was sold for use on the mainland in 1918.

On Monday 26th April 1883 the Isle of Wight Railway locomotive *Bonchurch*, a Beyer Peacock 2-4-0 tank, the sixth and largest new locomotive for the IWR, was being conveyed across the Solent. The tug and its barge encountered heavy seas off St. Helens, causing the barge to capsize and sink, taking the 35-ton locomotive with it. They were both salvaged on April 30th, the loco being landed at St. Helens.

Bonchurch was taken to Ryde Depot, for cleaning, and entered traffic on June 1st. In 1923 it was taken over by the Southern Railway and numbered W18, it was withdrawn in May 1928 and scrapped. During its career it had covered 1,326,067 miles, not a bad record for a 45 year old locomotive-that can't swim!